# First World War
### and Army of Occupation
# War Diary
### France, Belgium and Germany

### 38 DIVISION
### Headquarters, Branches and Services
### General Staff
### 1 August 1916 - 30 June 1917

### WO95/2540/1

The Naval & Military Press Ltd
www.nmarchive.com
Published in association with The National Archives

Published by

## The Naval & Military Press Ltd

Unit 10 Ridgewood Industrial Park,

Uckfield, East Sussex,

TN22 5QE England

Tel: +44 (0) 1825 749494

www.naval-military-press.com

www.nmarchive.com

*This diary has been reprinted in facsimile from the original. Any imperfections are inevitably reproduced and the quality may fall short of modern type and cartographic standards.*

**© Crown Copyright**
**Images reproduced by permission of The National Archives, London, England, 2015.**

# Contents

| Document type | Place/Title | Date From | Date To |
|---|---|---|---|
| Heading | 38th Division General Staff Aug 1916-Feb 1919 | | |
| Miscellaneous | A The National Archives | 06/07/2006 | 06/07/2006 |
| War Diary | Esquelbecq | 01/08/1916 | 20/08/1916 |
| War Diary | St Sixte | 21/08/1916 | 31/08/1916 |
| Operation(al) Order(s) | 38th (Welsh) Division Order No. 50 Appendix I | 01/08/1916 | 01/08/1916 |
| Operation(al) Order(s) | 38th (Welsh) Division Order No. 51. Appendix I.a. | 01/08/1916 | 01/08/1916 |
| Miscellaneous | Table Of Moves To Accompany 38th Order No. 51 | | |
| Operation(al) Order(s) | 38th (Welsh) Division Order No. 52 Appendix 2 | 03/08/1916 | 03/08/1916 |
| Miscellaneous | 38 Division No. G.121. App. 2.a. | 03/08/1916 | 03/08/1916 |
| Miscellaneous | 38th Div: No. G.204. App 3 | 04/08/1916 | 04/08/1916 |
| Operation(al) Order(s) | 38th (Welsh) Division Order No. 53. App. 4 | 06/08/1916 | 06/08/1916 |
| Miscellaneous | 38th Div. No. G. 463. App. 5 | 10/08/1916 | 10/08/1916 |
| Operation(al) Order(s) | 38th (Welsh) Division Order No. 54. App. 5a | 13/08/1916 | 13/08/1916 |
| Miscellaneous | March Table To Accompany Order No. 54 | | |
| Operation(al) Order(s) | 38th (Welsh) Division Order No. 55 App 6 | 19/08/1916 | 19/08/1916 |
| Miscellaneous | Train And March Table For Move Of 115th Infantry Brigade | 19/08/1916 | 19/08/1916 |
| Operation(al) Order(s) | 38th (Welsh) Division Order No. 56 App. 7 | 20/08/1916 | 20/08/1916 |
| Operation(al) Order(s) | 38th (Welsh) Division Order No. 57. App. 8 | 28/08/1916 | 28/08/1916 |
| Operation(al) Order(s) | Move Table To Accompany Order No. 50 | | |
| Heading | War Diary. General Staff 38th Division 1st To 31st August 1916 Volume IX Feb 19 | | |
| War Diary | St Sixte | 01/09/1916 | 30/09/1916 |
| Operation(al) Order(s) | 38th (Welsh) Division Order No. 58 App. I | 02/09/1916 | 02/09/1916 |
| Operation(al) Order(s) | Amendment To 38th (Welsh) Division Order No. 58 App. II | 06/09/1916 | 06/09/1916 |
| Miscellaneous | Table To Accompany 38th Division Order No. 58 Appendix 'A' | | |
| Miscellaneous | Table To Accompany 38th Division Order No. 58 Appendix 'B' | | |
| Operation(al) Order(s) | 38th (Welsh) Division Order No. 59 App. III | 14/09/1916 | 14/09/1916 |
| Operation(al) Order(s) | 38th (Welsh) Division Order No. 62. App. V | 16/09/1916 | 16/09/1916 |
| Operation(al) Order(s) | 38th (Welsh) Division Order No. 60 App. IV | 15/09/1916 | 15/09/1916 |
| War Diary | St Sixte | 01/10/1916 | 31/10/1916 |
| Operation(al) Order(s) | Amendment To 38th Division Order No. 63 App. I | 01/10/1916 | 01/10/1916 |
| Operation(al) Order(s) | 38th (Welsh) Division Order No. 63. App. I | 01/10/1916 | 01/10/1916 |
| Operation(al) Order(s) | 38th (Welsh) Division Order No. 64. App. II | 12/10/1916 | 12/10/1916 |
| Operation(al) Order(s) | 38th (Welsh) Division Order No. 65 App III | 22/10/1916 | 22/10/1916 |
| Operation(al) Order(s) | 38th (Welsh) Division Order No. 66 App IV | 31/10/1916 | 31/10/1916 |
| War Diary | St Sixte | 01/11/1916 | 30/11/1916 |
| Operation(al) Order(s) | 38th (Welsh) Division Order No. 67 Appendix 1 | 03/11/1916 | 03/11/1916 |
| Operation(al) Order(s) | 38th (Welsh) Division Order No. 68 Appendix 2 | 10/11/1916 | 10/11/1916 |
| Operation(al) Order(s) | 38th (Welsh) Division Order No. 69. Appendix 3 | 15/11/1916 | 15/11/1916 |
| Operation(al) Order(s) | 38th (Welsh) Division Order No. 70 App. 4 | 21/11/1916 | 21/11/1916 |
| Operation(al) Order(s) | 38th (Welsh) Division Order No. 70 Appendix 4 | 21/11/1916 | 21/11/1916 |
| Operation(al) Order(s) | 38th (Welsh) Division Order No. 71 Appendix 5 | 26/11/1916 | 26/11/1916 |
| Miscellaneous | March Table (To Accompany 38th Division Order No. 71) | | |
| Operation(al) Order(s) | 38th (Welsh) Division Order No. 71 Appendix 5 | 26/11/1916 | 26/11/1916 |
| Miscellaneous | 38th Division No. G.S. 1149 113th Brigade. | 17/11/1916 | 17/11/1916 |

| Type | Description | Start | End |
|---|---|---|---|
| Operation(al) Order(s) | 38th (Welsh) Division Order No. 69 | 15/11/1916 | 15/11/1916 |
| Miscellaneous | To:- Headquarters, 38th (Welsh) Division. | 27/11/1916 | 27/11/1916 |
| Operation(al) Order(s) | Amendment To 38th (Welsh) Division Order No. 72 | 30/11/1916 | 30/11/1916 |
| Operation(al) Order(s) | 38th (Welsh) Division Order No. 72 Appen 6 | 30/11/1916 | 30/11/1916 |
| Miscellaneous | March Table (To Accompany 38th Division Order No. 71) | | |
| Miscellaneous | | 26/11/1916 | 26/11/1916 |
| Miscellaneous | | | |
| War Diary | St Sixte. | 01/12/1916 | 14/12/1916 |
| War Diary | Esquelbecq. | 15/12/1916 | 31/12/1916 |
| Operation(al) Order(s) | 38th (Welsh) Division Order No. 73 App. I | 01/12/1916 | 01/12/1916 |
| Operation(al) Order(s) | 38th (Welsh) Division Order No. 74. App II | 09/12/1916 | 09/12/1916 |
| Miscellaneous | Move Table (To Accompany 38th (Welsh) Division Order No. 74) | 09/12/1916 | 09/12/1916 |
| Heading | 38th Division Important Not To Be Shown To Visitors | | |
| Heading | P.A. In 38th Division G.S. December 1915. Not To Be Available For Visitors. | | |
| Miscellaneous | C.2 Precis Report No. 117, Page 3, No. 1115 | | |
| Heading | Cover for Documents. Nature of Enclosures. S.S.143./E 38th Divn: Orders & Instsns | | |
| Heading | General Staff. 38th Division January 1917. Vol. 14 | | |
| War Diary | Esquelbecq | 01/01/1917 | 15/01/1917 |
| War Diary | And St. Sixte | 16/01/1917 | 31/01/1917 |
| Heading | War Diary Of General Staff 38th (Welsh) Division Volume XV February 1917 | | |
| War Diary | St Sixte. | 01/02/1917 | 28/02/1917 |
| Miscellaneous | 38th Division No. G.S. 4160 VIII Corps Report On Raid By The Germans On C.14.9 On The Night 24th/25th February 1917 | 24/02/1917 | 24/02/1917 |
| Heading | S.S. 143./G. 38th Div. Arty Instructions Orders | | |
| Heading | General Staff, 38th Division April 19 Vol. 16 | | |
| Heading | On His Majesty's Service. | | |
| War Diary | St Sixte | 01/03/1917 | 31/03/1917 |
| Heading | General Staff, 38th Division April 1917 Vol 17 | | |
| Heading | Cover for Documents. Nature of Enclosures. S.S. 143/K. XIII Corps Orders & Instrns | | |
| War Diary | St Sixte. | 01/04/1917 | 30/04/1917 |
| Miscellaneous | Fifth Army G.H.Q. G.H./2015 | 05/04/1917 | 05/04/1917 |
| Heading | General Staff, 38th Division. May 1917 Vol. 18 | | |
| Heading | S.S. 143/F III Corps Artillery Instructions. | | |
| Heading | Cover for Documents. Nature of Enclosures. Destroy I.E.M. | | |
| War Diary | St Sixte | 17/05/1917 | 31/05/1917 |
| War Diary | St Sixte. | 01/05/1917 | 15/05/1917 |
| Miscellaneous | Headquarters, 114 Infantry Brigade. | 02/05/1917 | 02/05/1917 |
| Miscellaneous | To:- Headquarters, 38th (Welsh) Division. | 04/05/1917 | 04/05/1917 |
| Miscellaneous | Report On Trenches Raided By 13th Bn. The Welsh Regt. Appendix D | | |
| Heading | Minor Operations Against Hindenburg Support Line, By 19 R. Welsh Fus., 119th Bde., 40th Div. On 15 December 1917 | | |
| Heading | General Staff, 38th Division. June 1917. Vol 19 | | |
| War Diary | St Sixte | 01/06/1917 | 08/06/1917 |
| War Diary | Dragon Camp | 09/06/1917 | 30/06/1917 |
| Operation(al) Order(s) | 38th Division No. G.S.S. 58/1. 38th (Welsh) Division Operations. Division Order No. 107. Addendum. | 15/06/1917 | 15/06/1917 |

# 38TH DIVISION

GENERAL STAFF

AUG 1916-FEB 1919

**TNA document reference:** WO 95/2540

The item(s) described below have been extracted from this document for reasons of preservation.

4 panoramic photographs showing 13th National Army Cantonment, Camp Dodge, Iowa

These extractions may now be ordered using

**document reference:** ...CN 4/20

Date: 6 July 2006

Signed: *Marion Edwards*

Name: Marion Edwards

# WAR DIARY
## INTELLIGENCE SUMMARY

*(Erase heading not required.)*

Army Form C. 2118

## VOLUME IX

| Place | Date | Hour | Summary of Events and Information | Remarks and references to Appendices |
|---|---|---|---|---|
| ESQUELBECQ | 1/8/16 | | In accordance with instructions issued by VIII Corps O.O. No.50. was issued. The 38th Divisional School was opened at VOLKERINCHOVE. Capt H.R. BENTLEY selected as commandant. G.O.51 issued. | Appendix 1. Appendix 1a |
| ESQUELBECQ | 2/8/16 | | 113 Bde group moved into camps in Squares F.27 + L.8 (20000 Sheet 27). G.O.C. + G.S.O.I. attended a demonstration at BERTHEM. | |
| ESQUELBECQ | 3/8/16 | | Under orders received from the VIII Corps certain units moved up into the forward area to work on the defensive lines. The 15th Welsh moved to TATINGHEM for employment by II Army School of Instruction. G.O.C. and G.S.O.I. reconnoitred the forward area. O.O. No.52 issued | Appendix 2. App. 2a. |
| ESQUELBECQ | 4/8/16 | | Conference at CHÂTEAU LOVIE VIII Corps Headquarters. G.O.C. G.S.O.I. + C.R.E. all attended. Continuation to O.O. 52. issued. | Appendix 3 |
| ESQUELBECQ | 5/8/16 | | Division in Corps Reserve, nothing to report. | |
| ESQUELBECQ | 6/8/16 | | Certain units moved. O.O. 53. issued. The Corps Commander Lt Gen. Sir A. HUNTER WESTON visited the 38th Divisional School at VOLKERINCHOVE. | Appendix 4 |
| ESQUELBECQ | 7/8/16 | | Nothing to report. Division in Corps Reserve. | |
| ESQUELBECQ | 8/8/16 | | " " | |
| ESQUELBECQ | 9/8/16 | | " " | |
| ESQUELBECQ | 10/8/16 | | Division in Reserve. G.S.O.I. reconnoitred part of the front to be taken over by 38th Division. | |

# WAR DIARY
## or
## INTELLIGENCE SUMMARY

*(Erase heading not required.)*

Army Form C. 2118

Instructions regarding War Diaries and Intelligence Summaries are contained in F.S. Regs, Part II. and the Staff Manual respectively. Title Pages will be prepared in manuscript.

| Place | Date | Hour | Summary of Events and Information | Remarks and references to Appendices |
|---|---|---|---|---|
| ESQUELBECQ | 11/8/16 | | Orders were received for 1 Battalion to move to BRANDHOEK. Remainder of Division in reserve. | Appendix 5 |
| ESQUELBECQ | 12/8/16 | | Division in Reserve. | |
| ESQUELBECQ | 13/8/16 | | Conference at VIII Corps Headquarters. G.O.C. G.S.O(i), A.A.&Q.M.G. C.R.E. & C.R.A. attended. The Divisional R.A. started to detrain in the 2nd Army area & billeted in the area LEDRINGHEM - ZEGGERS CAPPEL - ESQUELBECQ. O.O. 54 issued | Appx. 5. A. |
| ESQUELBECQ | 14/8/16 | | G.S.O(i) reconnoitred the front of the northern division (4th) in the VIII Corps front with a view to a relief. 114 Bde H'Qrs moved to POPERINGHE. | |
| ESQUELBECQ | 15/8/16 | | VIII Corps front with a view to a relief. Division in Reserve. | |
| ESQUELBECQ | 16/8/16 | | Conference at VIII Corps Headquarters. G.O.C. + G.S.O(i) attended. Orders received from the Corps to start relieving the 4th Division | Appendix 6 |
| ESQUELBECQ | 17/8/16 | | next day. O.O. 55 issued. | |
| ESQUELBECQ | 18/8/16 | 9 p.m. | 115 Bde moved by train from BOLLEZEELE area to relieve 11 Bde in the night sector the same night. G.O.C. proceeded to VIII Corps Headquarters for a conference. | |
| ESQUELBECQ | 19/8/16 | | 113 Bde relieved 10 Infantry Brigade in the left Sector. O.O. 56 issued. | Appendix 7 |
| ESQUELBECQ | 20/8/16 | | Divisional HQrs closed at ESQUELBECQ 10. a.m. & opened St SIXTE | |
| St SIXTE | 21/8/16 | | Noon. Relief of 4th Division continued. G.O.C. 38 Division | |

# WAR DIARY or INTELLIGENCE SUMMARY

Army Form C. 2118

(Erase heading not required.)

| Place | Date | Hour | Summary of Events and Information | Remarks and references to Appendices |
|---|---|---|---|---|
| ST SIXTE | 21/8/16 | | took over command of the line at 10 a.m. Relief of 4th Division R.A. continued. | |
| ST SIXTE | 22/8/16 | | Situation normal. Relief of 4th Divisional R.A. continued. | |
| ST SIXTE | 23/8/16 | | Situation normal. Relief of 4th Division complete. | |
| ST SIXTE | 24/8/16 | | Situation normal. | |
| ST SIXTE | 25/8/16 | | Situation normal. G.O.C. inspected front line trenches of the division. Situation | |
| ST SIXTE | 26/8/16 | | G.O.C. inspected front line trenches of the division. Situation normal. | |
| ST SIXTE | 27/8/16 | | Orders received for 15 Welsh Regt to rejoin the division. Situation normal. Brig. Gen. H.J. EVANS relinquished command of 115 Bde & proceeded to England. Brig. Gen. T.O. MARDEN took over command temporarily. Quiet day. | Appendix B |
| ST SIXTE | 28/8/16 | | Brig. Gen. T.O. MARDEN took over command of 115 Bde & proceeded to report. O.O. 67 issued. Quiet day. | |
| ST SIXTE | 29/8/16 | | Situation normal. | |
| ST SIXTE | 30/8/16 | | Conference at VIII Corps Headquarters. G.O.C. & S.O.I. Brig. Gen. C.J. HICKIE took over command of 115 Bde. Weather very bad. SIGNALS: Quiet day, addressed the Officers & | |
| ST SIXTE | 31/8/16 | | G.O.C. visited 38 Divisional School & addressed the Officers & M.C.Os. Slight artillery activity by the enemy against our front line trenches. Trenches in a very bad condition after the rain. | |

G.P.L. Drake Brockman
Captain
G.S.O. 38 Division

2-9-1916

Appendix I

COPY NO 23

S E C R E T

## 38TH (WELSH) DIVISION ORDER NO. 50

Reference :- Sheet 27.
              1/40,000.
                                        1st August 1916.

1. Moves will take place as shewn on attached table.
2. The Division is in Corps Reserve.
3. DIVISION HEADQUARTERS remain at ESQUELBECQ.
4. Completion of moves will be reported to DIVISIONAL HEADQUARTERS.

ACKNOWLEDGE

Arthur F. Smith
Capt.
for Lieut. Colonel,
General Staff, 38th (Welsh) Division.

Issued at :- 7.a.m.

Copies to :-

| | | |
|---|---|---|
| G.O.C. | A.D.M.S. | VIII Corps |
| G.S. | Div. Train | A.D.P.S. VIII Corps |
| "Q" | A.D.V.S. | R.T.O. ARNEKE |
| Signals | D.A.D.O.S. | |
| B.R.E. | A.P.M. | |
| 113th Brigade | S.S.O. | |
| 114th Brigade | Camp Comndt. | |
| 115th Brigade | 38th Sub-Park | |
| 19th Welsh Regt. | 38th Supply Col. | |

SECRET                                              COPY NO. 19

## 38TH (WELSH) DIVISION ORDER NO. 51.

Reference :- Sheets 27 and 28
              1/40,000                              1st August 1916.

1. In the event of the VIII Corps being attacked the 38th (Welsh) Division, which is in Corps Reserve, will concentrate in the area immediately West of POPERINGHE as in the attached Move Table.

2. The broad outline of the moves is as follows :-

    DIVISIONAL H.Q. from ESQUELBECQ to house at L.3.b.,3.5 about 1½ miles West of POPERINGHE.

    113TH INFANTRY BDE by road from HOUTKERQUE to Camps M and N in Square F.27.

    114TH INFANTRY BDE by bus from BOLLEZEELE to Area B in Squares F.25. and 26.

    115TH INFANTRY BDE by light railway from WULVERDINGHE and MILLAIN to Camps K and L in Square L.3.

    R.E. Coys. (less 1 Secn. each with their affiliated Brigade) move by Road to HOUTKERQUE.

    Pioneers remain at HOUTKERQUE.

    Field Ambulances (less a detachment from each with their affiliated Brigade) will concentrate at WATOU.

    A.S.C.Coys. will concentrate just East of WATOU.

3. All Units will be prepared to move in two hours time after receiving a telegram "DEFENCE SCHEME PREPARE". Moves will be carried out on receipt of a telegram to move.

4. A.P.M. will arrange for Traffic from East to West along the BOLLEZEELE, ESQUELBECQ, WORMHOUDT, HOUTKERQUE Road being diverted while the busses for the 114th Infantry Brigade are moving Eastwards.

5. Further details will be issued when action has to be taken.

    ACKNOWLEDGE

                                      H.E. Pryce
                                      Lieut. Colonel,
                            General Staff, 38th (Welsh) Divn.

Issued at :- 12-15 p.m.

Copies to :- (See overpage)

Issued at :- 12-15 p.m.

Copies to :-

| | |
|---|---|
| G.O.C. | A.D.M.S. |
| G.S. | Div. Train |
| "Q" | A.D.V.S. |
| Signals | D.A.D.O.S. |
| C.R.E. | A.P.M. |
| 113th Brigade | S.S.O. |
| 114th Brigade | Camp Commdt. |
| 115th Brigade | 38th Supply Col. |
| 19th Welsh Regt. | VIII Corps. |

SECRET   TABLE OF MOVES (TO ACCOMPANY 38TH ORDER NO. 5)

| UNIT | FROM | TO | VIA | REMARKS |
|---|---|---|---|---|
| 113th Brigade | HOUTKERQUE AREA | Camps M and N in F.27. | WATOU, ST. JAN-TER-BIEZON | (a) Will march under orders of G.O.C. 113th Inf. Bde. |
| 1 Sec. 123 Fd. Co.R.E. (a) | LEDRINGHEM | --ditto-- | --ditto-- | (b) Of such strength as A.D.M.S. considers necessary. |
| Detchmt 129th Fd. Amb. (a) (b) | HERZEELE | Camps M and N | --ditto-- | |
| 129th Fd. Amb. less detachment (a) | HERZEELE | Area E (WATOU) | WATOU | |
| 331st Coy. ASC. (a) | HOUTKERQUE | Area D which is just East of WATOU | WATOU | |
| 114th Brigade (c)(d) | BOLLEZEELE AREA | Area B in Squares F.25 and 26. | WORMHOUDT HERZEELE WATOU | (c) Will move under orders of G.O.C. 114th Brigade |
| | | | ST. JAN-TER-BIEZON. | (d) Will move by lorry. 40 lorries at a time will be available. Starting point the Church BOLLEZEELE. |
| 1 Sec. 124th Fd.Co.R.E. (c)(d) | VOLKERINGHOVE | --ditto-- | --ditto-- | --ditto-- |
| Detchmt. 130th Fd. Amb (c)(d) | --ditto-- | --ditto-- | --ditto-- | --ditto-- |
| 130th Fd. Amb. less detachment (c)(e) | --ditto-- | Area E (WATOU) | WORMHOUDT HERZEELE | (e) Will move by road |
| 332nd Coy. ASC (c)(e) | BOLLEZEELE | Area D | WATOU | |
| 115th Brigade (f) | WULVERDINGHE AREA | Camps K and L in Square L.3. | By light railway | (f) 8th Corps will arrange trains. |
| 1 Sec. 151st Fd.Co. (f) | MILLAIN | --ditto-- | --ditto-- | |
| Detachment 131st Fd. Ambulance (f) | MILLAIN | --ditto-- | --ditto-- | |
| 131st Fd. Amb. less detachment (g) | MILLAIN | AREA E (WATOU) | By road BOLLEZEELE WORMHOUDT WATOU | (g) Will march under their own orders. |
| 333rd Coy. ASC (g) | MILLAIN | AREA D | --ditto-- | |

## TABLE OF MOVES (Continued)

Page 2

| UNIT | FROM | TO | VIA | REMARKS |
|---|---|---|---|---|
| Div. Headquarters | ESQUELBECQ | L.3.b.,3.5 | WORMHOUDT HERZEELE HOUTKERQUE WATOU | By road |
| Sec. S.A.A. D.A.C. | WATTEN | AREA F in Squares E.23 and 24. | HOUTKERQUE | By road |
| Field Coys. R.E. | Present billets | HOUTKERQUE | By shortest route | To follow their Bde. Groups. |

S E C R E T

*War Diary Appendix 2*

COPY NO 24

## 38TH (WELSH) DIVISION ORDER NO. 52

Reference :- 1/40,000 Sheets 27 & 28          3rd August 1916.

1. Following move took place this morning :-
   15th Welsh Regiment from BOLLEZEELE to Second Army Central School of Instruction at TATINGHEM (two miles West of ST. OMER) instead of proceeding to WORMHOUDT (see Divisional Order No. 50).

2. Following moves took place this afternoon :-
   124th Field Coy. R.E. from VOLKERINCKHOVE to WORMHOUDT.
   151st Field Coy. R.E. from MILLAIN to WORMHOUDT.

3. Following moves will take place to-morrow :-

   (a) 124th Field Coy. R.E. will move from WORMHOUDT to ELVERDINGHE. They will complete the defence of that village.
   Officer Commanding Company has received detailed instructions from Headquarters, VIII Corps.

   (b) 2 Companies, 19th (Pioneer) Battalion Welsh Regiment and 2 Sections 151st Field Coy. R.E. will move from Camp F and WORMHOUDT respectively to YPRES, where they will work under the orders of the 29th Division. Billeting parties will report in advance to the Town Major.

   (c) One Company of Infantry from the 113th Infantry Brigade will move from K, L, M, N Camps to each of Works L.4 (H.11.b and d., H.12.a. and c, Sheet 28) and L.8. (H.5, Sheet 28). They will be accommodated in dugouts in these works, and will keep the works in good repair. These two Companies may not be relieved without previous reference to DIVISIONAL HEADQUARTERS.

4. On August 5th two Companies 19th (Pioneer) Battalion, Welsh Regiment, and two Sections 151st Field Coy. R.E. will move from WORMHOUDT to a place to be notified later to work under orders of 4th Division.
   An Officer from each of the two Pioneer Companies, and an Officer from each of the two R.E. Sections will report for instructions at the office of the C.R.E. Headquarters, 4th Division (Convent at A.1.d., 2.4, Sheet 28) at 11 a.m. to-morrow (August 4th).

5. Headquarters of 19th (Pioneer) Battalion Welsh Regiment will remain at Camp F.

6. Headquarters, 151st Field Coy. R.E. will accompany the two Sections proceeding to work under 4th Division.

A C K N O W L E D G E.

Arthur F. Smith, Captn.
for Lieut. Colonel,
General Staff, 38th (Welsh) Divn.

Issued at 7 p.m.
Copies to :- (See overpage)

Issued at :- 7 p.m.
Copies to :-

| | | |
|---|---|---|
| G.O.C. | A.D.M.S. | VIII Corps |
| G.S. | Div. Train | A.D.P.S. VIII Corps |
| "Q" | A.D.V.S. | R.T.O. ARNEKE |
| Signals | D.A.D.O.S. | 4th Division |
| C.R.E. | A.P.M. | 29th Division. |
| 113th Brigade | S.S.O. | |
| 114th Brigade | Camp Commdt | |
| 115th Brigade | 38th Sub-Park | |
| 19th Welsh Regt. | 38th Supply Col. | |

app. 2a.

38 Division No.G.121.

**114th Brigade.**
----------------

      Detail one Battalion to proceed to-day to Second Army Central School, of Instruction at TATINGHEM (2miles W. of ST OMER) instead of proceeding to WORMHOUDT area AAA This Battalion is required to help with the training and to be drilled at Army SchoolAAA Battalion must be clear of present billets by time Battalion of 115th Brigade which are coming into the billets arrives unless you can arrange direct with 115th Brigade for their incoming Battalion to arrive later AAA Under present orders they should arrive about 6.0.p.m.AAA Battalion you select must not arrive at TATINGHEM before 2.0.p.m. AAA Send billeting party on to TATINGHEM in morning AAA Report by return of D.R. which Battalion you detail AAA

38 Division.                                    (Sd) ARTHUR F SMITH, Capt,
S.D.R.12.25.a.m.                          for Lt Col,G.S.
3-8-16.

app: 3

SECRET.                                    38th Div: No. G. 204.

C.R.E.           A.D.M.S.        "Q"
19th Welsh Regt. Train           4th Divn.
113th Brigade    A.D.V.S.
114th Brigade    D.A.D.O.S.
115th Brigade    A.P.M..
Signals.         S.S.O.

---

Reference 1/40,000 Map, Sheet 28.

Reference 38th Division Order No. 52 para. 4.

1. The 2 Companies 19th (Pioneer) Battalion Welsh Regt and 2 Sections 151st Field Company R.E. will be accommodated on the CANAL BANK.

2. Forward billeting parties of above will report to the Staff Captain 11th Infantry Brigade at C.19.c.2.3.

3. The 2 Companies Pioneers should reach ELVERDINGHE by 11.p.m., where billeting parties will meet them there and guide them to CANAL BANK.

4. The 2 Sections R.E. should reach the ASYLUM in H.12.b. by 11.p.m., where billeting party will meet them, and guide them to CANAL BANK.

5. Transport of the Pioneers will bivouac at G.4.b. (with 1st Bn. King's Own, R.Lan.Regt.)

6. Transport of 2 Sections R.E. will bivouac at A.23.b.5.7.

7. Troops will not cross the VLAMMERTINGHE - ELVERDINGHE road before dusk August 5th.

Arthur F. Smith
Captain
for Lieut. Colonel,
General Staff, 38th (Welsh) Division.

4th August 1916.

*A/O: 4*
*War Diary*

SECRET.                                                          Copy No. 24

## 38TH (WELSH) DIVISION ORDER NO. 53.

                                                               6th August 1916.
Reference 1/40,000 Sheet 28.
------------------------------

1. The 10th Battn. Welsh Regt., less the last draft of 75 men will march today at any time to be selected by G.O.C., 114th Inf.Brigade to Camp N, F.21.c.3.0. where they will work under orders of 177th Tunnelling Company R.E.

2. 113th Inf. Brigade will readjust the position of their Battalions so as to leave room in Camp N for 10th Battn. Welsh Regt.

3. Details of accommodation will be arranged direct between 113th and 114th Infantry Brigades.

4. Baggage and Supply Wagons will accompany the Battalion, which will leve rationed up to and for August 7th.

5. 10th Battn. Welsh Regt.(less 75 men) will be attached to 113th Inf.Brigade for rations from August 8th.

6. The last draft of 75 men will remain behind and be attached to 13th Battn. Welsh Regt.

7. Orders re work will be issued to 10th Battn Welsh Regt later.

    ACKNOWLEDGE

                                            *Arthur F. Smith*
                                            *Captain*
                                            *for* Lieut. Colonel,
                                General Staff, 38th (Welsh) Division.

Issued at 7.a.m.

Copiestto :-

| G.O.C. | A.D.M.S. | 177th Tunnelling |
| G.S. | Div: Train | Company R.E. |
| "Q" | A.D.V.S. | R.T.O. ARNEKE |
| Signals | D.A.D.O.S. | A.D.P.S. VIII Corps |
| C.R.E. | A.P.M. | |
| 113th Brigade | S.S.O. | |
| 114th Brigade | Camp Comdt. | |
| 115th Brigade | 38th Supply Col. | |
| 19th Welsh Regt. | VIII Corps | |

C O P Y.   app: 5

38th Div: No. G. 463.

SECRET.

114th Brigade
(All units)

     Under telegraphic orders which have been issued separately the 14th Battn. Welsh Regt. will move from KRUGSTRAETE to BRANDHOEK tomorrow 11th instant arriving at the latter place in the afternoon and will be placed at the disposal of the 29th Division for carrying out the Corps buried Cable System.

                     (sd) ARTHUR F. SMITH.

                               Captain,
                                 for
                         Lieut. Colonel,
                         General Staff,
10th August 1916.        38th (Welsh) Division.

BRANDHOEK - Sq.G.12., Sheet 28.

App: 5a

SECRET.                                                            Copy No. 30

## 38TH (WELSH) DIVISION ORDER NO. 54.

13th August 1916.

Ref: Sheets 27 & 28 1/40,000.

1. Moves as per attached March Table will be carried out on Monday August 14th.

2. On completion of move the garrisons of the various works will be employed on the improvement of the defences of their work under the supervision of the R.E. Officers in charge of L. line of defences. The C.E. will see that these Officers are put in touch with the various garrisons.

3. Not more than 25% of the garrison of any post may be away from the post at any one time.

4. A small advanced party will proceed in the morning to each work etc. A bus for this party will be : in the SQUARE WORMHOUDT at 10.a.m.

5. Infantry will proceed from WORMHOUDT by train to POPERINGHE, and thence by march route.
   Trains for Infantry personnel leave as under :-

   |  | departs WORMHOUDT | arrives POPERINGHE |
   |---|---|---|
   | 1st Train | 17.08. | 19.47. |
   | 2nd Train | 17.18. | 19.57. |
   | 3rd Train | 17.28. | 20.07. |
   | 4th Train | 17.38. | 20.17. |

   Each train holds 225 persons.

   114th Brigade will arrange for the garrison of ELVERDINGHE to proceed by the first two trains.

6. Transport will proceed by road. Transport will not arrive at ELVERDINGHE or be East of LAMERTINGHE before 9.p.m. (N.B. Officers' chargers will proceed by road to meet trains at POPERINGHE station)

7. Portion of 13th Welsh Regt. moving to ELVERDINGHE will be rationed by 4th Division from 16th instant inclusive.

8. Portions of 13th Welsh Regt moving into L.4. and L.8 works will be rationed by 29th Division from 16th inclusive.

9. 2 Companies of 113th Brigade moving from L.4 and L.8 works to K.L.M.N. Camps area will be rationed by their Units from 16th instant inclusive.

10. Completion of moves will be reported to Divisional Headquarters.

ACKNOWLEDGE.

Arthur F. Smith Capt.
for Lieut. Colonel,
General Staff, 38th (Welsh) Division.

Issued at 7.p.m.
Copies to :-

| G.O.C. | 115th Bde. | Camp Comdt. |
| G.S. | 19th Welsh Rgt. | Supply Col. |
| "Q" | A.D.M.S. | VIII Corps |
| Signals | Train | 4th Divn. |
| C.R.E. | A.D.V.S. | 29th Divn. |
| C.R.A. | D.A.D.O.S. | R.T.O. ARNEKE |
| 113th Brigade | A.P.M. | A.D.P.S. VIII Corps |
| 114th Brigade | S.S.O. |  |

S E C R E T.    MARCH TABLE TO ACCOMPANY ORDER NO. 54.

| Unit | Move from | To | And relieve | Who proceed to | Remarks |
|---|---|---|---|---|---|
| 1 Coy. 13th Welsh 1 L.G. Regt. | KINKEN PUT | L. 4 Work (H.11.b c d) (H.12.a c c) | 1 Coy 115th Brigade | K.L.I.M. Camps Area. | Coy. 115th Brigade will not move till relieved. |
| 1 L.G. 15th Welsh Regiment | - ditto - | L. 3 Work (BRIELEN J.29) | (Nobody) | - | - |
| 2 platns)13th Welsh 1 L.G. ) Regt. | - ditto - | L. 8. Work (H.5.b.) | 1 Coy. 115th Brigade. | K.L.I.M Camps Area. | Coy 115th Bde. will not move till relieved. |
| 2 plns. 13th Welsh | - ditto - | POPERINGHE | (nobody) | | |
| 13 Welsh Regt (less 2 Coys & 5 L.G's) | - ditto - | ELVERDINGHE | 1 Bn. (less 2 Coys) 4th Divn. | | |
| 2 secs. 114th M.G. Company | - ditto - | - ditto - | - ditto - | | |
| 114th Bde. H.Q. | WORMHOUDT ) | POPERINGHE | (Nobody) | | |
| 114th M.G.Coy. (less 2 secs) | BOESENDAEL ) | | | | |
| 114th T.M.Bty. | WORMHOUDT ) | | | | |

S E C R E T                                                                  COPY NO. 36

app: 6

### 38TH (WELSH) DIVISION ORDER NO. 55

Reference :- Sheets 27 and 28                  August 19th 1916

1. The 38th (Welsh) Division will relieve the 4th Division in the Left Sector on the nights of 19th/20th and 20th/21st August.

2. The 115th Infantry Brigade will relieve the 12th Infantry Brigade in the Right Section on the night of 19th/20th August (see attached train and march table), details of relief will be arranged direct between Brigadiers concerned. Brigade Headquarters, CANAL BANK, C.25.d.,2.4.

3. The 113th Infantry Brigade will relieve the 10th Infantry Brigade in the Left Section on the night of 20th/21st August. Details will be arranged direct between Brigadiers concerned. Brigade Headquarters, CANAL BANK, C.19.c.,3.2. 2 busses to take advanced party who are going round the trenches will be at PROVEN at 10 a.m.

4. The 114th Infantry Brigade, on completion of move of the night 20th/21st August, detailed in 38th Division No. G.743 of the 18th instant, will be distributed as under :-

   Two ½ Battalions in L. Line

   Two ½ Battalions at BRANDHOEK working on Cable Trenches.

   One Battalion in Camp "N" working with 177th Tunnelling Coy.

   One Battalion at 2nd Army Central School of Instruction.

5. The Artillery of the 38th (Welsh) Division will relieve that of the 4th Division on the nights of 21st/22nd and 22nd/23rd August; the guns of the 4th Division being taken over by the personnel of the 38th Division. All details will be arranged direct between G.O's.C.,R.A. concerned.

6. The two Companies 19th (Pioneer) Battalion Welsh Regiment and two Sections, 151st Field Coy. R.E. at present attached to the 29th Division, will move on August 20th to Camp "F" where they will come under the orders of the 38th (Welsh) Division. The other two Companies, 19th (Pioneer) Battn. Welsh Regiment, and the other two Sections 151st Field Coy. R.E. now attached to the 4th Division will remain at CANAL BANK, and come under the orders of the 38th Division.

7. The 124th Field Coy. R.E. will remain at ELVERDINGHE, and will come under the orders of the 38th Division.

8. 38th Division Field Ambulances will relieve the Field Ambulances of the 4th Division under arrangements to be made between A.D's.M.S. concerned.

9.

Page 2.

9. The 38th Divisional School of Instruction will remain at VOLKERINCKHOVE for the present.

10. Further orders will be issued regarding move of Ammunition Sub-Park, A.D.V.S, DIVISIONAL HEADQUARTERS etc.

ACKNOWLEDGE

Issued at 7 a.m.

Arthur F. Smith Capt.
for Lieut. Colonel
General Staff, 38th (Welsh) Division.

Copies to :-

| | | |
|---|---|---|
| G.O.C. | 19th Welsh Regt. | VIII Corps |
| G.S. | A.D.M.S. | 4th Division |
| "Q" | Train | 29th Division |
| Signals | A.D.V.S. | 177th Tunnellg Coy.R.E. |
| C.R.E. | D.A.D.O.S. | 38th Div. School. |
| C.R.A. | A.P.M. | R.T.O. ARNEKE |
| 113th Brigade | S.S.O. | R.T.O. POPERINGHE |
| 114th Brigade | Camp Commdt. | R.T.O. HAZEBROUCK |
| 115th Brigade | Supply Column | A.D.P.S. VIII Corps. |

TRAIN AND MARCH TABLE FOR MOVE OF
115TH INFANTRY BRIGADE

To accompany 38th (Welsh) Division Order No. 35

| DATE | TRAIN DEPARTS BOLLEZEELE | NUMBER OF PASSENGERS | ARRIVES POPERINGHE |
|---|---|---|---|
| Aug. 19th. | 9 a.m. | 400 | About noon |
| | 9.10 a.m. | 400 | About 12.10 p.m. |
| | 9.20 a.m. | 200 | About 12.20 p.m. |
| | 9.30 a.m. | 200 | About 12.30 p.m. |
| | 9.40 a.m. | 200 | About 12.40 p.m. |
| | 9.50 a.m. | 200 | About 12.50 p.m. |
| | 10 a.m. | 200 | About 1 p.m. |
| | 4 p.m. | 200 | About 7 p.m. |
| | 4.10 p.m. | 200 | About 7.10 p.m. |
| | 4.20 p.m. | 200 | About 7.20 p.m. |
| | 4.30 p.m. | 200 | About 7.30 p.m. |
| | 4.40 p.m. | 200 | About 7.40 p.m. |

General Officer Commanding, 115th Infantry Brigade will arrange for that portion of his Brigade which goes by morning trains to bivouac between POPERINGHE and VLAMERTINGHE. No troops are to be East of VLAMERTINGHE before 8.45 p.m.

1st Line Transport will march brigaded under orders of General Officer Commanding, 115th Infantry Brigade.

2 Busses to take advanced party who are going round the trenches will be at BOLLEZEELE at 8 a.m.

Arthur F. Smith
Capt.
for Lieut. Colonel,
General Staff, 38th (Welsh) Division.

S E C R E T                                              COPY NO. 31

App: Y.

## 38TH (WELSH) DIVISION ORDER NO. 56

Reference :- Sheets 27 and 28.                    20th August 1916.

1. Two Companies, 19th (Pioneer) Battalion Welsh Regiment, at present attached to 29th Division, instead of moving to Camp "F" on 20th instant as per Division Order No. 55, will proceed to TROIS TOURS (B.28) on 20th instant, arriving there at 9 p.m. and relieving two Companies 4th Division Pioneers. One of these two Companies will take over the work of the Renfrew Field Coy. R.E. on night 21st/22nd under orders of C.R.E. 38th Division.

2. 151st Field Coy. R.E. will relieve the 9th Field Coy. R.E. on night 20th/21st; and will work in Right Brigade Area.

3. 124th Field Coy. R.E. will relieve Durham Coy. R.E. and one Company 19th (Pioneer) Battalion Welsh Regiment will relieve Renfrew Coy. R.E. both on night 21st/22nd. Details will be arranged between C.R.E's. concerned.
124th Field Coy. R.E. will work in Left Brigade Area.

4. At least three Sections each of 151st Field Coy. R.E. and 124th Field Coy. R.E. will be in CANAL BANK.

5. 19th (Pioneer) Battalion Welsh Regiment will supply C.R.E. with 20 men for supervision of Civilian Labour at POPERINGHE.

6. The Section 123rd Field Coy. R.E. will remain at BOLLEZEELE.

7. Field Ambulances will move on morning of 21st instant, taking over billets as follows :-

    129th Field Ambce - A.23.a., 2.0
    130th Field Ambce - PROVEN
    131st Field Ambce - A.28.a., 2.7.
    77th San. Section - A.14.d., 7.5.

    Trains for personnel and patients will leave as follows :-
                                                  Passengers
    Train 1. ⎧ Departs HERCKEGHEM 9 a.m.    150 personnel ⎫ F.A.
             ⎪                               20 patients  ⎪
             ⎨ Calls  ESQUELBECQ 9.45 a.m    35 personnel   San. Sec.
             ⎪
             ⎩ Arrives POPERINGHE about noon.

    Train 2. ⎧ Departs WORMHOUDT 9 a.m.     150 personnel ⎫ F.A.
             ⎨                              100 patients  ⎭
             ⎩ Arrives POPERINGHE about 10.45 a.m.

8. 49th Mobile Veterinary Section will move to K.5.d., 8.7 on morning of 21st instant.

9. Headquarters R.E. will move to ST. SIXTE (A.1.d., 1.2, Sheet 28) on morning of 21st instant.

10. Headquarters, 38th Divisional Train will move to ST. JEAN - TER - BIEZEN morning of 21st instant. Headquarter Co
    H.Q. Coy. 330th A.S.C. will move to F.25.a.)
    331st Coy. A.S.C.      will move to F.26.a.)
    332nd Coy. A.S.C.      will move to F.26.c.) On morning
    333rd Coy. A.S.C.      will move to F.27.b.) of 21st inst.

Page 2

11. 114th Infantry Brigade will arrange for 1 N.C.O. and 3 men to be at each of the following Posts at 4 p.m. to-day (20th instant) :-

P.7, 8, 9, 10.
G.1, 2, 3, 4, 5, 6, 7, 8.

Their duties will be to keep them in repair and improve the defences, and to prevent pilfering.

12. DIVISIONAL HEADQUARTERS will move to ST. SIXTE morning of 21st instant.

General Officer Commanding, 38th Division will assume Command of the Left Sector, VIII Corps at 10 a.m. 21st August at which hour DIVISIONAL HEADQUARTERS close at ESQUELBECQ and open at ST. SIXTE.

A C K N O W L E D G E

Arthur F. Smith
Captain
for Lieut. Colonel,
General Staff, 38th (Welsh) Division.

Issued at :- 7 a.m.

Copies to :-

| | | |
|---|---|---|
| G.O.C. | 19th Welsh Regt. | Sub-Park |
| G.S. | A.D.M.S. | VIII Corps |
| "Q" | Train | 4th Division |
| Signals | A.D.V.S. | 29th Division |
| C.R.E. | D.A.D.O.S. | 177th Tunnelling Coy. R.E. |
| C.R.A. | A.P.M. | 38th Divisional School |
| 113th Brigade | S.S.O. | R.T.O., ARNEKE |
| 114th Brigade | Camp Commdt. | R.T.O., POPERINGHE |
| 115th Brigade | Supply Column | A.D.P.S, VIII Corps. |

SECRET                                                    Copy No. 26

*app: 8.*

## 38TH (WELSH) DIVISION ORDER No. 57.

Reference Sheets :- B.5.a. 1/100,000                28th August 1916
                   28.N.W. 1/20,000

1. The 15th Battalion Welsh Regiment will rejoin the Division tomorrow the 29th instant. It will move from WISQUES to Camp "D" as under :-

      LEAVE                            ARRIVE
ST. MOMELIN in two trains           POPERINGHE at 13.07
at 8-50.a.m. and 9.am.               and 13-17.

The Battalion will then march via Cross Roads (G.5.d.1.2½) - Camp "D".

2. Transport will proceed by road via CASSEL where it will halt for the night 29th/30th August, leaving it at 5.a.m. on the 30th August so as to arrive early in Camp "D".

3. The Battalion (less transport and horses) will be rationed up to the 29th August, and the transport and horses up to the 30th August by the 2nd Army School.

4. On arrival at Camp "D" the Battalion will come under the orders of the G.O.C. 114th Infantry Brigade.

5. Completion of move to be reported to Divisional Headquarters.

ACKNOWLEDGE

*H.E. Pryce*

                                                         Lieut. Colonel,
Issued at 6-45.p.m.       General Staff, 38th (Welsh) Division.

Copies to :-

| | | |
|---|---|---|
| G.O.C. | 19th Welsh Regt. | Sub-Park. |
| G.S. | A.D.M.S. | VIII Corps |
| "Q" | Train | A.D.P.S. VIII Corps |
| Signals | A.D.V.S. | R.T.O. POPERINGHE |
| C.R.E. | D.A.D.O.S. | R.T.O. ST. MOMELIN |
| C.R.A. | A.P.M. | 38th Div: School. |
| 113th Brigade | S.S.O. | 29th Divn. |
| 114th Brigade | Camp Comdt. | |
| 115th Brigade. | Supply Column. | |

S E C R E T.  MOVE TABLE TO ACCOMPANY ORDER NO. 50.

| Date | UNIT | FROM | TO | ROUTE | |
|---|---|---|---|---|---|
| Aug. 2nd. | 113th Bde. (less 1 Bn.) | HERZEELE and HOUTKERQUE AREA | Camps K.L. M and N | ST.JAN-tor-BIEZEN | Brigade H.Q. to PROVEN. F.7.b. To reach Camps at 4.p.m. and occupy them as they are vacated by the 71st Brigade. Arrangements to be made direct with 71st Brigade (H.Q.PROVEN). |
| Aug. 2nd | 19th Welsh Regiment | HOUTKERQUE | Camp F. | -ditto- | To arrive 6.p.m. |
| 3rd | 1 Bn. 113th Brigade | HERZEELE & HOUTKERQUE Area | Camps K.L. M.N. | -ditto- | To march at 6.a.m. |
| | 123rd Fd.Co. R.E. | LEDRINGHEM | Camps K.L. M.N. | -ditto- | To march at 6.a.m. |
| | 129th Fd.Amb. | HERZEELE | F.29.b. | -ditto- | During morning. |
| | 331 Coy. ASC | HOUTKERQUE | F.29.c. | -ditto- | During morning. |
| | 114th Brigade Group. | BOLLEZEELE Area. | WORMHOUDT | Direct | (During morning (If there is not sufficient room in WORMHOUDT, troops may be billeted in HERZEELE. → move during morning |
| | 115th Brigade Group. | MILLAIN Area | BOLLEZEELE | Direct | |

NOTE :- POSITIONS OF CAMPS    Camp K.   L.3.d.. 7.4.
                              Camp L.   L.3.d.. 1.5.
                              Camp M.   F.27.c. 2.6.
                              Camp N.   F.21.c. 3.0.
                              Camp F.   A.18.c. central.

Confidential

38/ G.S. Vol 9

## WAR DIARY.

General Staff, 38th Division

1st to 31st August 1916

## VOLUME IX

Original Copy

Feb. '19

**WAR DIARY**
**INTELLIGENCE SUMMARY**
*(Erase heading not required.)*

Army Form C. 2118

General Staff 38th Divn

Volume X    Vol. 1    38

| Place | Date | Hour | Summary of Events and Information | Remarks and references to Appendices |
|---|---|---|---|---|
| ST SIXTE | 1/9/16 | | Situation normal | Appendix 1 |
| | 2/9/16 | | Situation normal. 0.0.58 carried re relief of 115 Bde by 114 Bde and 113 Bde by 115 Bde | |
| | 3/9/16 | | Situation normal | |
| | 4/9/16 | | G.O.C. inspected trenches of the left sector. Notting to report. | |
| | 5/9/16 | | The Corps Commander Sir. A. Hunter Weston visited the trenches of the left Bde. There was a conference at VIII Corps H.Qrs at CHATEAU LOVIE at 6.30 p.m. G.O.C. C.RA. & GSO.1. attended. A.S.O.1. G.O.C. + C.R.E. attended. | Appendix 2. |
| | 6/9/16 | | Amendment to 00.56 issued to discuss the question of drainage. Situation normal to 00.58. at VIII Corps HQrs. Situation normal | |
| | 7/9/16 | 11pm | Bde reliefs completed according to 00.58. Enemy endeavoured to raid our trenches at C.14.A.4. but was beaten off. Hostile trench mortar bombardment by the enemy previous to raid. | |
| | 8/9/16 | | Situation quiet. | |
| | 9/9/16 | | Nothing to report. | |
| | 10/9/16 | | Slight shelling of our trenches in C.14.A.d. Situation otherwise normal | |

# WAR DIARY
## or
## INTELLIGENCE SUMMARY
*(Erase heading not required.)*

Army Form C. 2118

| Place | Date | Hour | Summary of Events and Information | Remarks and references to Appendices |
|---|---|---|---|---|
| ST SYLVE | 11/9/16 | | Situation normal. Nothing to report. | |
| " | 12/9/16 | | Situation quiet. The War Minister The Rt. Hon. D. Lloyd George visited HQrs 38 Division. Situation normal | Appendix 3 |
| " | 13/9/16 | | Nothing to report. | |
| " | 14/9/16 | | O.O. 59 issued. G.O.C. visited raiding party of 13. R.W.F. O.O. 60 issued. Situation normal. | Appendix 4 |
| " | 15/9/16 | | 113 Bde started to relieve 115 Bde. Situation normal | |
| " | 16/9/16 | | Unsuccessful raid by 11.S.W.B. on CANADIAN DUGOUTS 60.62 nnnd Relief of 115 Bde by 113 Bde completed. Situation quiet. | Appendix 6 |
| " | 17/9/16 | | Situation normal | |
| " | 18/9/16 | | Unsuccessful raid by 13 R.W.F. G.O.C. 38 Div. + G.O.C. VIII Corps inspected trenches in the morning. Situation normal. | |
| " | 19/9/16 | | | |
| " | 20/9/16 | | G.O.C. presided at a conference of all Brigade + Battalion commanders at REIGERSBURG CHÂTEAU | |

Army Form C. 2118

# WAR DIARY
## or
## INTELLIGENCE SUMMARY
*(Erase heading not required.)*

Instructions regarding War Diaries and Intelligence Summaries are contained in F.S. Regs., Part II. and the Staff Manual respectively. Title Pages will be prepared in manuscript.

| Place | Date | Hour | Summary of Events and Information | Remarks and references to Appendices |
|---|---|---|---|---|
| St SIXTE | 21/9/16 | | Situation quiet | |
| „ | 22/9/16 | | Situation normal. Two German 1st Guard Reserve Regt entered trench | |
| „ | 23/9/16 | | Situation normal | |
| „ | 24/9/16 | | Situation normal | |
| „ | 25/9/16 | | Situation normal | |
| „ | 26/9/16 | | Situation quiet | |
| „ | 27/9/16 | | Nothing to report. Situation normal | |
| „ | 28/9/16 | | Situation normal. Successful raid by 13.RWF on the enemy's trenches in C.14.a. At 2.25 Raiding party of 11 SWB's entered the enemy trench. Nothing to report. Raiding party of 11 SWB's entered the enemy trench. | |
| „ | 29/9/16 | | Nothing to report but found them all empty. CANADIAN DUGOUTS | |
| „ | 30/9/16 | | Slight increase in hostile artillery fire, situation otherwise normal. | |

G.P.L Drake-Brockman
Capt
for Lt Col GS 38 Div

App. I

S E C R E T                                                  COPY NO 34

38TH (WELSH) DIVISION ORDER NO. 58

Reference :- 1/40,000 Sheets 27 & 28           2nd September 1916

1. (a) On September 4th, 114th Infantry Brigade will
   concentrate in the Reserve Brigade Area, viz Camps D.E.
   F. and P.  Moves will be carried out in accordance with
   Appendix 'A'.

   (b) 10 Battalion Welsh Regiment will remain at Camp "N"
   attached to 177th Tunnelling Company R.E.
   2nd Battalion Essex Regiment (4th Division) will be
   attached to the 114th Infantry Brigade (in place of
   10th Battalion Welsh Regiment) from September 4th.
   /st Line Transport of this Battalion will proceed to
   G.5.a., reporting to Brigade Transport Officer, 114th
   Infantry Brigade.

2. On nights September 5th/6th and 6th/7th 114th Infantry
   Brigade will relieve the 115th Infantry Brigade in Right
   Section, 115th Infantry Brigade will relieve 113th Inf.
   Brigade in Left Section, and 113th Infantry Brigade will
   move into the Reserve Brigade Area.  Moves will be
   carried out in accordance with Appendix 'B'.  All details
   will be arranged direct between Brigadiers concerned.

3. Two half Battalions of 4th Division (1st King's Own and
   2nd Lancashire Fusiliers) which will relieve the two
   half Battalions of 114th Infantry Brigade at BRANDHOEK
   will be employed nightly on burying cable in 38th Division
   Area from night September 4th/5th inclusive.

4. Headquarters 19th (Pioneer) Battalion Welsh Regiment will
   move to PELISSIER FARM (B.21.a.,1.1) on September 4th,
   and will be clear of Camp "F" by 10 a.m.

5. Two Companies 21st (Pioneer) Battalion West Yorkshire
   Regiment will be attached to the Division.  They will
   be accommodated in L.8 Work, arriving there after dark
   on September 8th.

6. 9th Field Company R.E. (less 1 Section), of 4th Division
   will move into ELVERDINGHE on September 8th, and take
   over work in the L Line (relieving 1 Section of 124th
   Field Company R.E.)  The transport of this Company will
   proceed to A.23.c.,4.5.

7. The 1/1st Durham Field Company R.E (less 1 Section) of the 4th Division will be attached to the 38th Division, arriving on September ~~4th~~, and will be accommodated as under :-

    1 Section at A.28.Central
    1 Section at A.15 b.,9.5.
    1 Section at TROIS TOURS A.28. (not to be East of the VLAMERTINGHE - ELVERDINGHE ROAD before 8.30 p.m.) This Section will be attached to the 19th (Pioneer) Bn, Welsh Regiment for rations, and will have its transport at A.15.b.,9.5.

8. Completion of moves and reliefs will be reported to DIVISIONAL HEADQUARTERS.

    A C K N O W L E D G E

Arthur F. Smith
Capt.
for Lieut. Colonel,
General Staff, 38th (Welsh) Divn.

Issued to Signals at 11 p.m.

Copies to :-

| | | |
|---|---|---|
| G.O.C. | 19th Welsh Regt. | Sub-Park |
| G.S. | A.D.M.S. | VIII Corps |
| "Q" | 38th Train | A.D.P.S. VIII Corps |
| Signals | A.D.V.S. | 4th Division |
| C.R.E. | D.A.D.O.S. | 29th Division |
| C.R.A. | A.P.M. | 5th Belgian Division |
| 113th Brigade | S.S.O. | R.T.O. POPERINGHE |
| 114th Brigade | Camp Commdt. | R.T.O. PESELHOEK |
| 115th Brigade | Supply Column | 38th Div. School. |

App. II

S E C R E T                       38th Division No. G.300

## AMENDMENT TO 38TH (WELSH) DIVISION ORDER NO.56

Reference 1/40,000 Sheets 27 & 28            6th Septr. 1916

<u>Para. 5</u>    Delete "September 7th" and substitute "Septr. 8th".

<u>Para. 6</u>    Delete "September 7th" and substitute "Septr. 8th".

<u>Para. 7</u>    Delete "September 7th" and substitute "Septr. 8th".

<u>A C K N O W L E D G E</u>

*H. E. Pryce*
Lieut. Colonel,
General Staff, 38th (Welsh) Division.

Copies to :-

| | | |
|---|---|---|
| G.O.C. | 19th Welsh Regt. | A.D.P.S. VIII Corps |
| G.S. | A.D.M.S. | 4th Division |
| "Q" | 38th Train | 29th Division |
| Signals | A.D.V.S. | 5th Belgian Division |
| C.R.E. | D.A.D.O.S. | R.T.O. POPERINGHE |
| C.R.A. | A.P.M. | 38th Div. School. |
| 113th Brigade | S.S.O. | |
| 114th Brigade | Camp Commdt | |
| 115th Brigade | VIII Corps | |

SECRET  APPENDIX 'A'

## TABLE TO ACCOMPANY 38TH DIVISION ORDER NO. 58

| Date | Unit | Move from | To | Remarks |
|---|---|---|---|---|
| 4-9-16. | 14th Welsh Regt. (Less 2 Coys.) | BRANDHOEK | Camp E. | To be clear of BRANDHOEK by 11 a.m |
| | 2 Coys. 14th Welsh | "L" Works | Camp E | Move on relief by 1st King's Own about 9.15 p.m. |
| | 13th Welsh Regt. (Less 2 Coys.) | ELVERDINGHE | Camp F. | Move on relief by 2nd Lancashire Fusiliers about 9 a.m. |
| | 2 Coys. 13th Welsh | BRANDHOEK | Camp F | To be clear of BRANDHOEK by 11 a.m |
| | 2nd Essex Regt. | POPERINGHE | Camp P | To arrive in Camp P about 11.30 a.m. where it will come under orders of G.O.C. 114th Brigade. |
| | 2 Sections, 114th M.G. Company | ELVERDINGHE | Reserve Bde. Area | Move on relief by 2 Sections of 4th Division about 9 a.m. |
| | 114th Brigade H.Q. | POPERINGHE | Camp "D" | Move in morning. |

S E C R E T     TABLE TO ACCOMPANY 38TH DIVISION ORDER NO. 58     APPENDIX 'B'

| Date Night | Unit | Move from | To | Relieving | Who proceed to | Remarks |
|---|---|---|---|---|---|---|
| Septr. 5th/6th. | 2 Battns. 114th Bde. | Reserve Brigade Area | Right Bde. Reserve. | 2 Battns. 115th Bde. | Left Brigade Reserve | |
| | 2 Battns. 115th Bde. | Right Brigade Reserve. | Left Bde. Reserve. | 2 Battns. 113th Bde. | Reserve Bde Area | 2 Battns 115th Bde will not move till relieved by 2 Battns 114th Brigade |
| | 2 Battns. 113th Bde. | Left Bde. Reserve. | Reserve Bde. Area | --- | --- | 2 Battns 113th Bde will not move till relieved by 2 Battns 115th Brigade. |
| Septr. 6th/7th. | 2 Battns. 114th Bde. | Reserve Bde. Area | Right Bde. Reserve. | 2 Battns 114th Bde. | Front line Right Bde. | |
| | 2 Battns. 114th Bde. | Right Bde. Reserve. | Front line Right Bde. | 2 Battns. 115th Bde. | Left Bde. Reserve. | 2 Battns. 114th Bde. will not move till relieved by 2 Battns. 114th Bde. G.O.C. 114th Bde will assume command Right Section on completion of relief. |
| | 2 Battns. 115th Bde. | Front line Right Bde. | Left Bde. Reserve | 2 Battns. 115th Bde. | Front line Left Bde. | |
| | 2 Battns. 115th Bde. | Left Bde. Reserve. | Front line Left Bde. | 2 Battns. 113th Bde. | Rsve. Bde. Area. | 2 Battns. 115th Bde. will not move till relieved by 2 Battns. 115th Bde. G.O.C. 115th Bde. will assume command of Left Section on completion of the relief. |
| | 2 Battns. 113th Bde. | Front line Left Bde. | Rsve. Bde. Area. | --- | --- | |

NOTE :- Relief of M.G.Coys. and T.M.Batteries will be arranged direct between Brigades.

Arthur F. Smith
Lieut. Colonel,
General Staff, 38th (Welsh) Division.

App: III

S E C R E T                                     COPY NO 28

## 38TH (WELSH) DIVISION ORDER NO. 59

Reference :- 1/40,000                           14th Septr. 1916.
             Sheet 28.

1. On nights 16th/17th and 17th/18th instant the 113th Infantry Brigade will relieve the 115th Infantry Brigade in the Left Section.
   All details will be arranged direct between Brigadiers concerned.

2. No formed bodies of 113th Infantry Brigade will be East of the VLAMERTINGHE - ELVERDINGHE ROAD before 8 p.m.

3. General Officer Commanding 113th Infantry Brigade will assume command on completion of relief which will be reported to DIVISIONAL HEADQUARTERS.

4. On relief the 115th Infantry Brigade will send one Platoon to the Divisional School at Camp "H", where they will be at the disposal of the Commandant, Divisional School for drill, fatigues etc.

Acknowledge

                                        Arthur F. Smith, Capt.
                                    for Lieut. Colonel,
                          General Staff, 38th (Welsh) Divn.

Issued to Signals at 7 p.m.

Copies to :-

| | | |
|---|---|---|
| G.O.C. | 19th Welsh Regt | A.D.P.S. VIII Corps |
| G.S. | A.D.M.S. | 4th Division |
| "Q" | 38th Train | 29th Division |
| Signals | A.D.V.S. | 5th Belgian Divn. |
| C.R.E. | D.A.D.O.S. | R.T.O. POPERINGHE |
| C.R.A. | A.P.M. | |
| 113th Infantry Brigade | S.S.O. | 38th Div. School. |
| 114th Infantry Brigade | Camp Commdt. | |
| 115th Infantry Brigade | VIII Corps | |

Opp: V

SECRET                                          Copy No. 25

## 38TH (WELSH) DIVISION ORDER NO. 62.

Ref: Maps, Sheets 27 & 28.                    16th September 1916.

1. Division Order No. 61 is cancelled.

2. One Battalion, 115th Infantry Brigade will tonight on relief by 113th Infantry Brigade move into Right Brigade Reserve under General Officer Commanding 114th Infantry Brigade in place of 2nd Essex Regt.

3. On completion of relief 115th Infantry Brigade will be located as under :-
   | | |
   |---|---|
   | Headquarters | Camp D |
   | 1 Battalion | Camp D |
   | 1 Battalion | Camp E |
   | 1 Battalion | Camp P |
   | 1 Battalion | Under G.O.C. Right Section. |
   | M.G.Coy. | Camp S. |

4. The Battalion proceeding to camp P will send one platoon to the Divisional School at Camp H.

5. The Battalions in D and E Camps will work on the CANAL BANK nightly commencing night 18th/19th, one Battalion in the Right and one Battalion in the Left Bde. Areas respectively.
   The Battalion at Camp P will work on horse standings in the back area under A.A. & Q.M.G., who will be notified by 115th Brigade of working strength available.

6. In the event of attack the "L" Works will be manned by the Brigade of 29th Division in Corps Reserve until the 7th Division take over the garrisons of these posts on joining VIII Corps.

7. Cable burying parties are suspended for the present.

8. Pioneers will cease work on THREADNEEDLE and HUDDERSFIELD but will otherwise continue work as at present.

9. All units, 4th Division working in 38th Division area will rejoin their Division by 10.a.m. September 17th.

ACKNOWLEDGE

Arthur F. Smith Capt.
for Lieut. Colonel,
General Staff, 38th (Welsh) Division.

Issued to Signals at 12.15 pm
Copies to :-
| | | |
|---|---|---|
| G.O.C. | 19th Welsh Regt. | VIII Corps |
| G.S. | A.D.M.S. | 4th Divn. |
| "Q" | Train | 29th Divn. |
| Signals | A.D.V.S. | R.T.O. POPERINGHE. |
| C.R.A. | D.A.D.O.S. | 1st King's Own |
| C.R.E. | A.P.M. | 2d Lan Fus |
| 113th Bde. | Camp Comdt. | |
| 114th Bde. | Div: School. | |
| 115th Bde. | 177th Tn:Co.,R.E. | |

SECRET    COPY NO. 36

App- IV

## 38TH (WELSH) DIVISION ORDER NO. 60

Reference :- Maps, Sheet 28, 1/20,000    15th September 1916.
              1/10,000

1. Certain operations, details regarding which have been communicated confidentially to those concerned, will take place to-night.

2. Zero hour will be 11 p.m.

3. The 29th Division may discharge gas between A.5.a., to A.7. at 11 p.m. to-night. Notices as to whether it will be discharged or not will be sent to Right and Left Infantry Brigades, and Right and Left Groups Artillery only. Infantry Brigades will inform other Units on the CANAL BANK in their respective areas.

4. All vehicles should be clear of YPRES and the YPRES - ELVERDINGHE ROAD on their return journey by 10.45 p.m.

5. There will be no working parties in the Left Brigade Area, nor at HILL TOP, GOWTHORPE ROAD and TURCO in the Right Brigade Area.
Work on the CANAL BANK is to be continued, except that no working parties will be furnished from the 113th Infantry Brigade.

6. A C K N O W L E D G E

H.E. Pryce
Lieut. Colonel,
General Staff, 38th (Welsh) Division.

Issued at :-
Copies to :-
| | | |
|---|---|---|
| G.O.C. | A.D.V.S. | 29th Division |
| G.S. | D.A.D.O.S. | 5th Belgian Div. |
| "Q" | A.P.M. | O.C. Permanent Garr: |
| Signals | 1st King's Own | ELVERDINGHE. |
| C.R.A. | 2nd Lan: Fus: | 24th H.A. Group |
| C.R.E. | D/R.M.A.,A.A.Bty. | Det. "J" Coy., 3rd |
| 113th Brigade | 10th Entrenching Bn. | Bn. Spec. Bde. R.E. |
| 114th Brigade | 4th Labour Bn. R.E. | Nos. 5 & 6 Sections |
| 115th Brigade | 1/1st Durham Fd.Co.,R.E. | 2nd Pontoon Park |
| 19th Welsh Regt. | 177th Tunnelling Co.,R.E. | TOWN MAJOR, |
| A.D.M.S. | 9th Field Co., R.E. | POPERINGHE. |
| 38th Div. Train | VIII Corps | |

VOLUME XI  OCTOBER 1916  Army Form C. 2118

**WAR DIARY**
of
~~INTELLIGENCE SUMMARY~~

Duplicate
General Staff
38th (Welsh) Division

| Place | Date | Hour | Summary of Events and Information | Remarks and references to Appendices |
|---|---|---|---|---|
| ST SIXTE | 1/10/16 | | Situation quiet. O.O. 63 issued with amendment. | Appendix 1 |
| " | 2/10/16 | | Situation normal | |
| " | 3/10/16 | | Slight artillery activity against left sector, situation otherwise quiet. | |
| " | 4/10/16 | | Relief of 115 Bde by 114 Bde & 113 Bde by 115 Bde completed. Situation normal. | |
| " | 5/10/16 | | Situation normal. | |
| " | 6/10/16 | | Some artillery activity against the left sector. | |
| " | 7/10/16 | | Sap 9 cleared of the enemy by a party of 10.S.W.B. Some trench mortar activity against the left Bde front. Situation otherwise normal. | |
| " | 8/10/16 | | Slight artillery activity against left sector | |
| " | 9/10/16 | | Slight artillery activity against COLNE VALLEY | |
| " | 10/10/16 | | Attempted enterprise against the CANADIAN DUGOUTS by 17. R.W.F. not successful. Situation normal. | |
| " | 11/10/16 | | Some activity by trench mortars on either side. Situation otherwise normal. | |

# WAR DIARY

## INTELLIGENCE SUMMARY

Army Form C. 2118

Instructions regarding War Diaries and Intelligence Summaries are contained in F.S. Regs., Part II. and the Staff Manual respectively. Title Pages will be prepared in manuscript.

| Place | Date | Hour | Summary of Events and Information | Remarks and references to Appendices |
|---|---|---|---|---|
| ST SIXTE. | 12/10/16 | | Situation normal. Successful raid by 13. R.W.F. on the enemy's trenches at C.14.a.4.2. One prisoner 2nd Grado Res Reg'to taken. Party 15 well raided MORTEDJE SAP but found no German rifle C.O. 64 comdt. the menagu sector. | Reg Maj B.E.G.O.M B.1/0000 Appendix |
| " | 13/10/16 | | Slight artillery activity against the menagu trenches. Successful raid by 15. R.W.F. against the hostile trenches at C.13.6.9.8. Four known belonging to the 1st Grand Reserve Regt taken. Unsuccessful raid by 13. Welsh against hostile trenches by SapIo. | |
| " | 14/10/16 | | Situation normal. | |
| " | 15/10/16 | | Some activity by our artillery. Hostile trench mortars active against left sector. | |
| " | 16/10/16 | | Slight hostile artillery activity against Left Bde. The 2nd ARMY COMMANDER. Lt-Gen. SIR. H. PLUMER. visited the CANAL BANK. the 71s Bde (in reserve). He also made a presentation of decorations to various officers, N.C.O.s + men. Slight artillery activity against Left Bde. Situation normal | |
| " | 17/10/16 | | Situation quiet. | |
| " | 18/10/16 | | Heavy rain all day resulting in damage to trenches. Bombardment by hostile artillery FT.M's damaging CAVAN TRENCH. | |
| " | 19/10/16 | | | |

# WAR DIARY or INTELLIGENCE SUMMARY

Army Form C. 2118

| Place | Date | Hour | Summary of Events and Information | Remarks and references to Appendices |
|---|---|---|---|---|
| St SIXTE. | 20/9/16 | | Situation normal. | |
| " | 21/9/16 | | Situation normal. Great aerial activity | |
| " | 22/9/16 | | Situation normal. Brig. Gen. T.O. MARDEN C.M.G. took over command of the division while the G.O.C. Maj. Gen. C.J. BLACKADER proceeded on leave to ENGLAND. D.O. issued | Appendix 3. |
| " | 23/9/16 | | Situation normal. There was a conference at CHÂTEAU LOVIE VIII Corps Headquarters 5.30 p.m. Brig.Gen. MARDEN, A.S.O.L. GRA. attended. | |
| " | 24/9/16 | | Situation quiet normal. | |
| " | 25/9/16 | | Situation normal. Relief of 115 Bde by 113 Bde expected. | |
| " | 26/9/16 | | Situation normal. Successful bombardment of the hostile trenches in C.7.C. carried out by artillery + trench mortars. | |
| " | 27/9/16 | | Situation normal. | |
| " | 28/9/16 | | Hostile artillery active against the trenches of the left Bde. Some damage done. | |
| " | 29/9/16 | | Some damage done to the trenches in the left Bde area. Successful raid by 16 R.W.F. on the hostile trenches of C.7.c. 5½.7¾. Three prisoners 86 Res. Regt. 18 Res. Division captured. | |

# WAR DIARY
## INTELLIGENCE SUMMARY

Army Form C. 2118

| Place | Date | Hour | Summary of Events and Information | Remarks and references to Appendices |
|---|---|---|---|---|
| S. SIXTE | 30/10/16 | | Situation normal | Appendix 4. |
| " | 31/10/16 | | Slight hostile artillery activity. Situation otherwise quiet. O.O. 66. issued | |
| | | | 13/11/16. | |
| | | | G.P.L. Drake-Brockman Cpr A.S. 38 (Welsh) Division | |

S E C R E T

App. I

## AMENDMENT TO 38TH DIVISION ORDER NO. 63

Ref: Map Sheet 28, 1/40,000                                    1st Octr. 1916

Delete Para. 7 and substitute :-

7. The 114th Infantry Brigade will not furnish working parties for the CANAL BANK or Buried Cable System on the nights of 2nd/3rd and 3rd/4th instant, but will provide them from the night of the 4th/5th instant as usual. The 115th Infantry Brigade will not work on Horse Standings on the 2nd and 3rd instant. The 114th Infantry Brigade will start work on the Horse Standings on the 5th instant.

A C K N O W L E D G E

G. Drake-Brockman
Capt.
for Lieut. Colonel,
General Staff, 38th (Welsh) Division.

Copies to :-

| | | |
|---|---|---|
| G.O.C. | 19th Welsh Regt. | VIII Corps |
| G.S. | A.D.M.S. | 29th Divn. |
| "Q" | Train | R.T.O., POPERINGHE |
| Signals | A.D.V.S. | Adjt. i/c Camps. |
| C.R.A. | D.A.D.O.S. | |
| C.R.E. | A.P.M. | |
| 113th Brigade | Camp Commdt. | |
| 114th Brigade | Div: School | |
| 115th Brigade | 177th Tun. Coy., R.E. | |

S E C R E T  

App. I  
Copy No. 25

## 38TH (WELSH) DIVISION ORDER NO. 63.

Ref: Map Sheet 28, 1/40,000                1st October 1916.

1. On the nights of the 2nd/3rd and 3rd/4th instant, the 115th Infantry Brigade will relieve the 114th Infantry Brigade in the Right Section. All details of relief will be arranged direct through Brigadiers concerned.

2. No formed bodies of the 115th Brigade will be East of the VLAMERTINGHE - ELVERDINGHE ROAD before 6-30.p.m.

3. The General Officer Commanding 115th Infantry Brigade will assume command on completion of relief which will be reported to Divisional Headquarters.

4. The 114th Infantry Brigade will send one platoon to relieve the platoon of the 16th Welsh Regt. now at the Divisional School (Camp H) on the morning of October 2nd.

5. Raiding parties of the 13th, 14th, and 15th Battns, Welsh Regt will remain at MACHINE GUN FARM (H.5.central) closing up so as to make room for the raiding parties of the 115th Infantry Brigade.

6. The Left Reserve Battalion of the 115th Infantry Brigade will be accommodated in the CANAL BANK, less Bn. H.Q. and 2 Coys at MACHINE GUN FARM.

7. There will be no work on the CANAL BANK or BURIED CABLE SYSTEM on the nights 2nd/3rd and 3rd/4th. Work will start again on the night of the 4th/5th as usual. The 115th Infantry Brigade will not work on horse standings on the 2nd and 3rd instant. The 114th Infantry Brigade will start work on the Horse Standings on the 5th instant.

    ACKNOWLEDGE

                               Capt  
                                 Lieut. Colonel,  
                General Staff, 38th (Welsh) Division.

Issued to Signals at 12 noon.

Copies to :-

| | | |
|---|---|---|
| G.O.C. | 19th Welsh Regt. | VIII Corps |
| G.S. | A.D.M.S. | 29th Divn. |
| "Q" | Train | R.T.O., PODERINGHE |
| Signals | A.D.V.S. | Adjt. i/c Camps. |
| C.R.A. | D.A.D.O.S. | |
| C.R.E. | A.P.M. | |
| 113th Brigade | Camp Comdt. | |
| 114th Brigade | Div: School | |
| 115th Brigade | 177th Tun. Coy., R.E. | |

App. II

SECRET                                                    Copy No. 25

### 38TH (WELSH) DIVISION ORDER NO. 64.

12th October 1916.

1. On nights 14th/15th, 15th/16th October, 114th Infantry Bde. (less 10th Welsh Regt) will relieve 115th Infantry Brigade in Right Section and 115th Infantry Bde. will relive 113th Infantry Brigade in Left Section.

2. No formed bodies of 114th Brigade will be East of the VLAMERTINGHE - ELVERDINGHE ROad before 5-15.p.m.

3. All details of the relief will be arranged direct between Brigadiers concerned.

4. On completion of relief General Officer Commanding 114th Brigade will assume command of the Right Section and the General Officer Commanding 115th Brigade of the Left Section.

5. 113th Infantry Brigade will detail one Battalion to be attached to 114th Brigade in place of 10th Welsh Regt.

6. The officer and 30 men of 13th Battn. Welsh Regt. now doing special cable burying work under A.D.A.S. VIII Corps will remain under the orders of the A.D.A.S., until the work is completed.

7. 113th Infantry Brigade will on relief detail a platoon to proceed to Camp H where it will come under orders of the Commandant Divisional School.

8. On nights 14th/15th and 15th/16th there will be no cable burying or work on CANAL BANK and STRONG POINTS. There will be no work on Horse Standings on 14th and 15th instant. 113th Brigade will start work on Horse Standings on 16th instant and will find cable burying party on and after night 16th/17th instant.

9. Completion of reliefs will be reported to Divisional Head Quarters.

    ACKNOWLEDGE

                                    Arthur F. Smith
                                            Captain,
                        General Staff, 38th (Welsh) Division.

Issued at 6-30.a.m.

Copies to :-
| | | | |
|---|---|---|---|
| G.O.C. | 113th Bde. | A.D.V.S. | VIII Corps |
| G.S. | 114th Bde. | D.A.D.O.S. | 55th Division |
| "Q" | 115th Bde. | A.P.M. | 5th Belgium Divn. |
| Signals | 19th Welsh | Camp Comdt. | R.T.O. POPERINGHE. |
| C.R.A. | A.D.M.S. | Div: School | Adjt. 1/cCamps. |
| C.R.E. | Train | 177th Tun.Co. | |

App: III

SECRET                                          COPY NO. 25

## 38TH (WELSH) DIVISION ORDER NO. 65

22nd October 1916

1. On nights 24/25th and 25/26th October, 113th Infantry Brigade will relieve the 115th Infantry Brigade in the Left Section.

2. 115th Infantry Brigade will place one Battalion at the disposal of the General Officer Commanding, 114th Infantry Brigade (in place of 10th Battalion Welsh Regiment).

3. All details of the relief will be arranged direct between Brigadiers concerned.

4. No formed bodies of the 113th Infantry Brigade will be East of the VLAMERTINGHE - ELVERDINGHE ROAD before 5 p.m.

5. The General Officer Commanding, 113th Infantry Brigade will assume command of the Left Section on completion of relief which will be reported to Divisional Headquarters.

6. The 115th Infantry Brigade will on relief detail one Platoon to proceed to Camp "H" where it will come under the orders of the Commandant, Divisional School.
The 115th Infantry Brigade will report to the Commandant, Divisional School direct the strength of the Platoon, and the time of arrival at the School.

7. On nights 24/25th and 25/26th October there will be no Cable Burying.
There will be no work on Horse Standings on 24th and 25th October.
The 115th Infantry Brigade will start work on Horse Standings on 26th instant, and will find cable burying party on and after night 26/27th October.

ACKNOWLEDGE

Arthur F. Smith Capt
for Lieut. Colonel,
General Staff, 38th (Welsh) Division.

Issued at 6.30 a.m.
Copies to :-

| G.O.C. | 19th Welsh Regt. | VIII Corps |
| G.S. | A.D.M.S. | 55th Division |
| "Q" | Train | 5th Belgian Divn. |
| Signals | A.D.V.S. | R.T.O. POPERINGHE. |
| O.R.A. | D.A.D.O.S. | Adjt. i/c Camps. |
| C.R.E. | A.P.M. | |
| 113th Brigade | Camp Commdt. | |
| 114th Brigade | Div. School | |
| 115th Brigade | 177th Tun. Coy., R.E. | |

App: IV

SECRET                                                          COPY NO 25

## 38TH (WELSH) DIVISION ORDER NO. 66

31st Octr. 1916

1. On night 4th/5th November, 115th Infantry Brigade (less one Battalion) will relieve 114th Infantry Brigade (less one Battalion) in the Right Section.
   The Battalion of the 115th Infantry Brigade left in Reserve Brigade Area will be accomodated in Camp "P" and will be under the orders of the General Officer Commanding, 114th Infantry Brigade.

2. The 114th Infantry Brigade will place one Battalion at the disposal of the General Officer Commanding, 115th Infantry Brigade, until the 9th November. On night November 9th/10th this Battalion will be relieved by the Battalion of the 115th Infantry Brigade in "P" Camp.

3. All details of relief will be arranged between Brigadiers concerned.

4. No formed bodies of the 115th Infantry Brigade will be East of the VLAMERTINGHE - ELVERDINGHE ROAD before 4.30 p.m.

5. The General Officer Commanding, 115th Infantry Brigade will assume command of the Right Section on completion of relief which will be reported to Divisional Headquarters.

6. The 114th Infantry Brigade will on relief detail one platoon to proceed to Camp "H" where it will come under the orders of the Commandant, Divisional School.

7. On night 4th/5th there will be no cable burying, and on the 4th November there will be no work on horse standings.
   114th Infantry Brigade will start work on horse standings on 5th November, and will find cable burying party on and after night 5th/6th.

   A C K N O W L E D G E

                                        Arthur F. Smith
                                             Capt.
                                       for  Lieut. Colonel,
                             General Staff, 38th (Welsh) Divn.

Issued at 6.30 a.m.
Copies to :-

| G.O.C. | 19th Welsh Regt. | VIII Corps |
| G.S. | A.D.M.S. | 55th Division |
| "Q" | Train | 5th Belgian Divn. |
| Signals | A.D.V.S. | R.T.O. POPERINGHE |
| C.R.A. | D.A.D.O.S. | Adjt. i/c Camps. |
| C.R.E. | A.P.M. | |
| 113th Brigade | Camp Commdt. | |
| 114th Brigade | Div. School | |
| 115th Brigade | 177th Tun.Coy.,R.E. | |

# WAR DIARY
## or
## INTELLIGENCE SUMMARY

(Erase heading not required.)

Army Form C. 2118

HQ GS 38 D
Vol 12

| Place | Date | Hour | Summary of Events and Information | Remarks and references to Appendices |
|---|---|---|---|---|
| ST SIXTE | 1/11/16 | | Some hostile artillery and trench mortar activity during the day. Amendment to O.O.64 (see O.O War Diary) | GDB |
| " | 2/11/16 | | Situation normal. G.O.C. Major-Gen. C.G. BLACKADER returned from leave in ENGLAND. | GDB Appendix 1 GDB |
| " | 3/11/16 | | Slight hostile trench mortar activity against EALING TRENCH. Brig-Gen. T.O. MARDEN resumed command of the 114 Bde. O.O.67 issued | GDB |
| " | 4/11/16 | | Slight hostile shelling of YSER CANAL BANK, ELVERDINGHE and RIVOLI FARM. H.R.H. the DUKE OF CONNAUGHT visited the 38 Divisional area in the morning. The G.O.C. 38 Division Major-Gen C.G. BLACKADER G.O.C. 113 Bde Brig-Gen L.A.E PRICE-DAVIES and G.O.C 114 Bde Brig-Gen T.O. MARDEN were presented to his Royal Highness. In the afternoon G.O.C. and G.S.O.1 visited the VIII Corps School near LOO. CHATEAU ROVIE. | GDB |
| " | 5/11/16 | | Slight hostile artillery activity against N Brigade front. The G.O.C. 2nd Army Commander Lt-Gen Sir H. PLUMER visited 38 Division HQrs. Commander 1st Army visited the trenches of the left Brigade | GDB |
| " | 6/11/16 | | G.O.C. & S.O.1 & C.R.E visited situation normal. | GDB GSO |
| " | 7/11/16 | | Situation quiet. Weather very wet in the morning. | GDB |
| " | 8/11/16 | | Nothing to report. Situation normal. | GDB |
| " | 9/11/16 | | Slight increase in hostile artillery fire. | GDB |

# WAR DIARY
or
## INTELLIGENCE SUMMARY

Army Form C. 2118

| Place | Date | Hour | Summary of Events and Information | Remarks and references to Appendices |
|---|---|---|---|---|
| ST SIXTE | 10/11/16 | | Slight hostile artillery and trench mortar activity against 4th Bde. Our trench mortars carried out a successful bombardment of the enemy's trenches in C.7.c. 1668 rounds were fired. 0.0 68 round Situation normal. The VIII Corps Commander Sir. AYLMER HUNTER WESTON visited Divisional HQrs. | ADS Appendix 2 ADR |
| " | 11/11/16 | | Situation normal. | ADR |
| " | 12/11/16 | | Situation quiet. | ADS |
| " | 13/11/16 | | Our Trench Mortars and artillery bombarded a Salient in the enemy's line known as CAESARS NOSE. 1297 rounds were fired. The VIII Heavy Artillery registered on HIGH COMMAND REDOUBT | ADS |
| " | 14/11/16 | | Relief of 116 Bde by 144 Bde. 115 Bde relieved 118 Bde in the left Sector. Situation normal. 00.69 issued. | ADB Appendix 3 ADB |
| " | 15/11/16 | | Bombardment of HIGH COMMAND REDOUBT by VIII Corps H.Art. and 39 Divl. Artillery. The G.O.C. 8th Corps Sir A. HUNTER WESTON attended. G.O.C. of 113 Bde. presented medals to units of 113 Bde. | |
| " | 16/11/16 | | Bombardment of HIGH COMMAND REDOUBT followed by raid by 7 officers and 150 O.R.s. Raid very successful resulting in capture of 4 M.G. + 20 men of 31 R.I.R. Much damage done by R.E. | ADB |
| " | 17/11/16 | | Hounr w/o contents dugouts + M.G. emplacements. | |

# WAR DIARY
## or
## INTELLIGENCE SUMMARY
*(Erase heading not required.)*

Army Form C. 2118

Instructions regarding War Diaries and Intelligence Summaries are contained in F.S. Regs., Part II. and the Staff Manual respectively. Title Pages will be prepared in manuscript.

| Place | Date | Hour | Summary of Events and Information | Remarks and references to Appendices |
|---|---|---|---|---|
| S<sup>t</sup> SIXTE | 18/4/16 | | Slight hostile artillery activity. | GDB |
| " | 19/4/16 | | The 8th Corps Commander Sir A. HUNTER WESTON inspected the raiding party of the 14th Welsh + congratulated them on their success. G.O.C. and representatives from R.E., R.A. and 2 Corps H. Art. attended. | GDB |
| " | 20/4/16 | | Situation normal. Officers from the 5th Belgian Division inspected the sniping by a Camp. H. G.O.C. 113, 114, 115 Bde attended at conference at Divisional HQrs. | GDB |
| " | 21/4/16 | | Situation quiet. The 8th Corps Commander Sir A HUNTER WESTON inspected the 38th Divisional School. A.S.O.1. proceeded to CHATEAU LOVIE + received instructions concerning relief of 174 French Territorial Bde in the sector B.12.b.4.4. to B.6.c.4.5. by a brigade of the 39th Division. Situation quiet. Appendix 4 | GDB |
| " | 22/4/16 | | G.O.C. and G.S.O.1. reconnoitred the Sector to be taken over. Station quiet. | |
| " | 23/4/16 | | Slight hostile shelling of LANCASHIRE FARM. Brig-Gen E. FINCH HATTON G.O.C. 118 Bde | |
| " | 24/4/16 | | Situation normal. Div HQrs visited. Div HQrs is taking over new sector. | |

Army Form C. 2118

# WAR DIARY
## or
## INTELLIGENCE SUMMARY
*(Erase heading not required.)*

Instructions regarding War Diaries and Intelligence Summaries are contained in F.S. Regs., Part II and the Staff Manual respectively. Title Pages will be prepared in manuscript.

| Place | Date | Hour | Summary of Events and Information | Remarks and references to Appendices |
|---|---|---|---|---|
| St SIXTE | 26/11/16 | | Situation normal. G.O.C. inspected the huts of 38 Div Sniping Coy. | ADB |
| " | 26/11/16 | 1·2 p.m. | Hostile artillery active against Div front. Div R.A. retaliated with good effect. O.O.71 issued | Appendix 5 |
| " | 27/11/16 | | Slight hostile hostile trench mortar activity against the M brigade front. The Second Army Commander Lt Gen. Sir H. PLUMER visited 38 Div Hdqrs. Enemy shelled front, support line heavily between 7.30 p.m. & 8.30 p.m. Damage slight; the enemy | ODB |
| " | 28/11/16 | | Our trench mortars successfully bombarded trenches in the vicinity of HAMPSHIRE FARM. | ADB |
| " | 29/11/16 | | Situation normal. The Trench Mortars cooperated in a raid by the 55th Division, by bombarding the hostile trenches near HAMPSHIRE FARM. | ODB |
| " | 30/11/16 | | Hostile artillery active against COLNE VALLEY and FARGATE. O.O.72 issued. The G.O.C. 8 Corps presented medals to units 115 Bde at D camp. G.O.C. and G.S.O.1 attended. | ADB / Appendix 6 |

A.T.L. Drake-Brockman
Capt
1/12/16 G.S. 38 Div

*Appendix 1.*

S E C R E T              COPY NO. 15

### 38TH (WELSH) DIVISION ORDER NO. 67

Reference :- Sheet 28 N.W.2., 1/10,000          3rd Novr. 1916

1. In retaliation for frequent Trench Mortaring of EALING TRENCH and its neighbourhood, a Trench Mortar bombardment will be carried out on CAKE TRENCH, CAKE SUPPORT and ESSEN FARM in the near future.

2. The bombardment will be carried out by "X" "Y" and "Z" Trench Mortar Batteries, and 113th, 114th and 115th Stokes Mortar Batteries supported by the Artillery.

3. The bombardment will be carried out under the orders of the G.O.C.,R.A. in conjunction with the General Officer Commanding, Left Infantry Brigade. Three copies of the orders will be submitted to Divisional Headquarters on the 6th instant.
Stokes Mortar Batteries will be under the orders of the Divisional Trench Mortar Officer for this bombardment.

4. Reconnaissances for positions etc. will be carried out on the 5th instant. Emplacements will be made on the 6th and 7th instant, and ammunition brought up on the night of the 7th instant.
The bombardment will be carried out on the 8th or 9th instant in the afternoon, the exact day to be settled later. The retaliation, if possible, will be carried out on the afternoon of a day on which the enemy Trench Mortar EALING TRENCH and its neighbourhood in the morning.

5. The General Officers Commanding, 113th and 115th Infantry Brigade will arrange for trenches being cleared as necessary during the bombardment.

6. On the night of the bombardment the General Officer Commanding, 113th Infantry Brigade will send out a strong fighting patrol or patrols to inflict damage on any patrols who may be expected to be on the flanks of the bombarded portion, ready to attack our probably expected raiding party.
A copy of the orders for this patrol or patrols should be submitted to Divisional Headquarters at an early date.
Arrangements will also be made by the General Officer Commanding, 113th Infantry Brigade for bringing Artillery, Machine Gun and Stokes Mortar fire on to enemy parties who may be out in "NO MAN'S LAND" near the point of bombardment.

7. Indirect Machine Gun fire should be brought on to damaged portions of the enemy's parapet when it is reported that working parties are there.

Page 2

8. The Divisional Sniping Officer will arrange for sniping posts being prepared in order to take advantage of opportunities that should present themselves after the bombardment.

9. As our heavy retaliation in the afternoon may cause a certain amount of heavy mortaring by the enemy a day or two after our bombardment, arrangements will also be made for repeating, if necessary, the bombardment when this takes place, and sending out fighting patrols again in the evening.

A C K N O W L E D G E

H. E. Pryce
Lieut. Colonel,
General Staff, 38th (Welsh) Division.

Issued at :- 7 p.m.

Copies to :-

| | |
|---|---|
| G.O.C. | 38th Div: T.M.O. |
| G.S. | 38th Div: Sniping Coy. |
| G.O.C., R.A. | C. R. E. |
| 113th Brigade | 19th Pioneers |
| 114th Brigade | 177th Tun: Coy. R.E. |
| 115th Brigade | No. 23 Kite Balloon Sec: |

Appen 1 War Diary

S E C R E T                                              COPY NO. 14


## 38TH (WELSH) DIVISION ORDER NO. 67

Reference :- Sheet 28 N.W.2., 1/10,000                3rd Novr. 1916

1. In retaliation for frequent Trench Mortaring of EALING TRENCH and its neighbourhood, a Trench Mortar bombardment will be carried out on CAKE TRENCH, CAKE SUPPORT and ESSEN FARM in the near future.

2. The bombardment will be carried out by "X" "Y" and "Z" Trench Mortar Batteries, and 113th, 114th and 115th Stokes Mortar Batteries supported by the Artillery.

3. The bombardment will be carried out under the orders of the G.O.C., R.A. in conjunction with the General Officer Commanding, Left Infantry Brigade. Three copies of the orders will be submitted to Divisional Headquarters on the 6th instant.
Stokes Mortar Batteries will be under the orders of the Divisional Trench Mortar Officer for this bombardment.

4. Reconnaissances for positions etc. will be carried out on the 5th instant. Emplacements will be made on the 6th and 7th instant, and ammunition brought up on the night of the 7th instant.
The bombardment will be carried out on the 8th or 9th instant in the afternoon, the exact day to be settled later. The retaliation, if possible, will be carried out on the afternoon of a day on which the enemy Trench Mortar EALING TRENCH and its neighbourhood in the morning.

5. The General Officers Commanding, 113th and 115th Infantry Brigade will arrange for trenches being cleared as necessary during the bombardment.

6. On the night of the bombardment the General Officer Commanding, 113th Infantry Brigade will send out a strong fighting patrol or patrols to inflict damage on any patrols who may be expected to be on the flanks of the bombarded portion, ready to attack our probably expected raiding party.
A copy of the orders for this patrol or patrols should be submitted to Divisional Headquarters at an early date.
Arrangements will also be made by the General Officer Commanding, 113th Infantry Brigade for bringing Artillery, Machine Gun and Stokes Mortar fire on to enemy parties who may be out in "NO MAN'S LAND" near the point of bombardment.

7. Indirect Machine Gun fire should be brought on to damaged portions of the enemy's parapet when it is reported that working parties are there.

Page 2

8. The Divisional Sniping Officer will arrange for sniping posts being prepared in order to take advantage of opportunities that should present themselves after the bombardment.

9. As our heavy retaliation in the afternoon may cause a certain amount of heavy mortaring by the enemy a day or two after our bombardment, arrangements will also be made for repeating, if necessary, the bombardment when this takes place, and sending out fighting patrols again in the evening.

A C K N O W L E D G E

H. E. Pryce
Lieut. Colonel,
General Staff, 38th (Welsh) Division.

Issued at :- 7 p.m.

Copies to :-

| | |
|---|---|
| G.O.C. | 38th Div: T.M.O. |
| G.S. | 38th Div: Sniping Coy. |
| G.O.C.,R.A. | C. R. E. |
| 113th Brigade | 19th Pioneers |
| 114th Brigade | 177th Tun: Coy. R.E. |
| 115th Brigade | No. 23 Kite Balloon Sec: |

Appen 2.

S E C R E T.                                     COPY NO. ___


38TH (WELSH) DIVISION ORDER NO. 68
_____

Reference :- Sheet 28 N.W.2., 1/10,000          10th Novr. 1916.


1. On nights of 14/15th and 15/16th November, 114th Infantry Brigade (less 10th Welsh Regiment) will relieve the 115th Infantry Brigade in the Right Section and 115th Infantry Brigade will relieve the 113th Infantry Brigade in the Left Section.

2. No formed bodies of 114th Brigade will be East of the VLAMERTINGHE – ELVERDINGHE Road before 4-30 p.m.

3. All details of the relief will be arranged direct between the Brigadiers concerned.

4. On completion of relief General Officer Commanding 114th Brigade will assume command of the Right Section and the General Officer Commanding 115th Brigade of the Left Section.

5. 113th Infantry Brigade will detail one Battalion to be attached to 114th Brigade in place of 10th Welsh Regt.,

6. 113th Infantry Brigade will on relief detail a platoon to proceed to Camp "H" where it will come under the orders of the Commandant Divisional School. The platoon from 114th Brigade now at the Divisional School will rejoin its unit on the 14th instant.

7. On the nights 14/15th and 15/16th there will be no cable burying. There will be no work on Horse Standings on 14th and 15th instant. The 113th Brigade will start work on Horse Standings on the 16th instant and will find cable burying parties on and after night 16/17th.

8. Completion of reliefs will be reported to Divisional Head Quarters.

A C K N O W L E D G E.

                                        Lieut Colonel,
                General Staff, 38th (Welsh) Division.
Issued at 1-30 p.m.

Copies to :-

| | | | |
|---|---|---|---|
| G.O.C. | 113th Bde. | A.D.V.S. | VIII Corps |
| G.S. | 114th Bde. | D.A.D.O.S. | 55th Division |
| "Q" | 115th Bde. | A.P.M. | 5th Belgian Div. |
| Signals | 19th Welsh | Camp Comdt. | R.T.O. POPERINGHE |
| C.R.A. | A.D.M.S. | Div: School | Adjt.i/c. Camps. |
| C.R.E. | Train. | 177th Tun.Co. | |

SECRET.  *Appen. 2* War Diary  COPY NO. ____

### 38TH (WELSH) DIVISION ORDER NO. 68

Reference :- Sheet 28 N.W.2., 1/10,000     10th Novr. 1916.

1. On nights of 14/15th and 15/16th November, 114th Infantry Brigade (less 10th Welsh Regiment) will relieve the 115th Infantry Brigade in the Right Section and 115th Infantry Brigade will relieve the 113th Infantry Brigade in the Left Section.

2. No formed bodies of 114th Brigade will be East of the VLAMERTINGHE – ELVERDINGHE Road before 4-30 p.m.

3. All details of the relief will be arranged direct between the Brigadiers concerned.

4. On completion of relief General Officer Commanding 114th Brigade will assume command of the Right Section and the General Officer Commanding 115th Brigade of the Left Section.

5. 113th Infantry Brigade will detail one Battalion to be attached to 114th Brigade in place of 10th Welsh Regt.,

6. 113th Infantry Brigade will on relief detail a platoon to proceed to Camp "H" where it will come under the orders of the Commandant Divisional School. The platoon from 114th Brigade now at the Divisional School will rejoin its unit on the 14th instant.

7. On the nights 14/15th and 15/16th there will be no cable burying. There will be no work on Horse Standings on 14th and 15th instant. The 113th Brigade will start work on Horse Standings on the 16th instant and will find cable burying parties on and after night 16/17th.

8. Completion of reliefs will be reported to Divisional Head Quarters.

A C K N O W L E D G E.

*A Derrymajor*
Lieut Colonel,
General Staff, 38th (Welsh) Division.

Issued at 1-30 p.m.

Copies to :-

| | | | |
|---|---|---|---|
| G.O.C. | 113th Bde. | A.D.V.S. | VIII Corps |
| G.S. | 114th Bde. | D.A.D.O.S. | 55th Division |
| "Q" | 115th Bde. | A.P.M. | 5th Belgian Div. |
| Signals | 19th Welsh | Camp Comdt. | R.T.O. POPERINGHE |
| C.R.A. | A.D.M.S. | Div: School | Adjt.i/c. Camps. |
| C.R.E. | Train. | 177th Tun.Co. | |

*Appen: 3.*

V E R Y
S E C R E T.

Copy No. 24

38TH (WELSH) DIVISION ORDER NO. 69.

15th November 1916.

1. A raid will be carried out by the 14th Battalion, Welsh Regiment on the night 17th/18th instant at a time and on an obective which have been communicated to the units concerned.

2. There will be no working or carrying parties North of CONEY STREET or East of BOUNDARY ROAD except such as General Officers Commanding 114th and 115th Brigades may order.

3. All horse transport must be West of the YPRES - ELVERDINGHE Road between 5-45.p.m. and 1.a.m. Motor lorries will be similarly restricted except those carrying the raiding party.

4. There will be no Buried Cable Working Party on the night 17th/18th instant.

PLEASE ACKNOWLEDGE

H. E. Pryce
Lieut. Colonel,
General Staff, 38th (Welsh) Division.

Issued to Signals at 6-30.p.m.

Copies to :-

| | | |
|---|---|---|
| G.O.C. | A.D.M.S. | VIII Corps |
| G.S. | Train | 55th Divn. |
| "Q" | A.D.V.S. | 5th Belgian Division. |
| Signals | D.A.D.O.S. | |
| C.R.A. | A.P.M. | |
| C.R.E. | Camp Comdt. | |
| 113th Bde. | Div: School | |
| 114th Bde. | 177th Tun.Coy. | |
| 115th Bde. | Corps O.P., Nos 3. | |
| 19th Welsh Regt. | | |

War Diary
Appen 3

V E R Y
S E C R E T.

Copy No. 23

### 38TH (WELSH) DIVISION ORDER NO. 69.

15th November 1916.

1. A raid will be carried out by the 14th Battalion, Welsh Regiment on the night 17th/18th instant at a time and on an objective which have been communicated to the units concerned.

2. There will be no working or carrying parties North of CONEY STREET or East of BOUNDARY ROAD except such as General Officers Commanding 114th and 115th Brigades may order.

3. All horse transport must be West of the YPRES - ELVERDINGHE Road between 5-45.p.m. and 1.a.m. Motor lorries will be similarly restricted except those carrying the raiding party.

4. There will be no Buried Cable Working Party on the night 17th/18th instant.

PLEASE ACKNOWLEDGE

H.E. Pryce
Lieut. Colonel,
General Staff, 38th (Welsh) Division.

Issued to Signals at 6-30.p.m.

Copies to :-

| | | |
|---|---|---|
| G.O.C. | A.D.M.S. | VIII Corps |
| G.S. | Train | 55th Divn. |
| "Q" | A.D.V.S. | 5th Belgian Division. |
| Signals | D.A.D.O.S. | |
| C.R.A. | A.P.M. | |
| C.R.E. | Camp Comdt. | |
| 113th Bde. | Div: School | |
| 114th Bde. | 177th Tun.Coy. | |
| 115th Bde. | Corps O.P., Nos 3. | |
| 19th Welsh Regt. | | |

SECRET                                                          COPY NO. 26

## 38TH (WELSH) DIVISION ORDER NO. 70

Reference :- Sheet 28 N.W.2, 1/10,000                    Novr. 21st 1916

1. The 113th Infantry Brigade will relieve the 115th Infantry Brigade in the Left Section on nights 24th/25th and 25th/26th November 1916.

2. The 115th Infantry Brigade will place one Battalion at the disposal of the General Officer Commanding, 114th Infantry Brigade (in place of the 10th Battalion The Welsh Regiment).

3. All details of the relief will be arranged direct between the Brigadiers concerned.

4. No formed bodies of the 113th Infantry Brigade will be East of the VLAMERTINGHE - ELVERDINGHE ROAD before 4.15 p.m.

5. The General Officer Commanding 113th Infantry Brigade will assume Command of the Left Section on completion of relief which will be reported to Divisional Headquarters.

6. The 115th Infantry Brigade will detail one Platoon to report at 4 p.m. on the 25th instant to the Commandant, Divisional School, "H" Camp.
The Platoon of the 113th Infantry Brigade now at the School will rejoin its Brigade during the morning of the 25th November.

7. On nights 24th/25th and 25th/26th November there will be no Cable Burying. There will be no work on Horse Standings on the 24th and 25th instant.
The 115th Infantry Brigade will start work on Horse Standings on the 26th instant, and will find Cable Burying Parties on and after the night 26th/27th Novr. 1916.

ACKNOWLEDGE

Lieut. Colonel,
General Staff, 38th (Welsh) Division.

Issued to Signals at 6.30 a.m.
Copies to :-

| | | |
|---|---|---|
| G.O.C. | 19th Welsh Regt. | VIII Corps |
| G.S. | A.D.M.S. | 55th Division |
| "Q" | Train | 5th Belgian Divn. |
| Signals | A.D.V.S. | 39th Division |
| C.R.A. | D.A.D.O.S. | R.T.O. POPERINGHE |
| C.R.E. | A.P.M. | Adjt. i/c Camps. |
| 113th Brigade | Camp Commdt. | |
| 114th Brigade | Div. School | |
| 115th Brigade | 177th Tun: Coy. R.E. | |

*War Diary*
*Appens 4*

SECRET                                              COPY NO. 25

### 38TH (WELSH) DIVISION ORDER NO. 70

Reference :- Sheet 28 N.W.2, 1/10,000                Novr. 21st 1916

1. The 113th Infantry Brigade will relieve the 115th Infantry Brigade in the Left Section on nights 24th/25th and 25th/26th November 1916.

2. The 115th Infantry Brigade will place one Battalion at the disposal of the General Officer Commanding, 114th Infantry Brigade (in place of the 10th Battalion The Welsh Regiment).

3. All details of the relief will be arranged direct between the Brigadiers concerned.

4. No formed bodies of the 113th Infantry Brigade will be East of the VLAMERTINGHE - ELVERDINGHE ROAD before 4.15 p.m.

5. The General Officer Commanding 113th Infantry Brigade will assume Command of the Left Section on completion of relief which will be reported to Divisional Headquarters.

6. The 115th Infantry Brigade will detail one Platoon to report at 4 p.m. on the 25th instant to the Commandant, Divisional School, "H" Camp.
   The Platoon of the 113th Infantry Brigade now at the School will rejoin its Brigade during the morning of the 25th November.

7. On nights 24th/25th and 25th/26th November there will be no Cable Burying. There will be no work on Horse Standings on the 24th and 25th instant.
   The 115th Infantry Brigade will start work on Horse Standings on the 26th instant, and will find Cable Burying Parties on and after the night 26th/27th Novr. 1916.

ACKNOWLEDGE

Lieut. Colonel,
General Staff, 38th (Welsh) Division.

Issued to Signals at 6.30 a.m.
Copies to :-

| | | |
|---|---|---|
| G.O.C. | 19th Welsh Regt. | VIII Corps |
| G.S. | A.D.M.S. | 55th Division |
| "Q" | Train | 5th Belgian Divn. |
| Signals | A.D.V.S. | 39th Division |
| C.R.A. | D.A.D.O.S. | R.T.O. POPERINGHE |
| C.R.E. | A.P.M. | Adjt. i/c Camps. |
| 113th Brigade | Camp Commdt. | |
| 114th Brigade | Div. School | |
| 115th Brigade | 177th Tun: Coy. R.E. | |

SECRET    COPY NO. 28

*Appen 5.*

# 38TH (WELSH) DIVISION ORDER NO. 71

Reference :- 1/20,000 Map, Sheet 28 N.W.
and Trench Maps                    26th November 1916.

1. The Sector now held by the French 79th Territorial Regiment will be taken over by the VIII Corps on the 29th and 30th November 1916.
   This Sector extends from the present left of the 38th Division to B.6.c.,½.5 (trench A.6 inclusive).
   The Boundary between VIII Corps and Belgians will be :-

   B.6.c.,½.5 (junction of trenches A.6 and A.7) - BOYAU DE LA CHAPELLE (inclusive to VIII Corps) - Road at B.5.d.,7.1 - junction of trenches C.5 and C.6 at B.11.a.,7.7 - Road at B.11.a.,2.6½ - Cross Roads at B.10.b.,1.3½ - BOYAU DE BOESINGHE at B.9.b.,8.0 - Road at B.9.a.,2.3½ - B.8.b.,6.3½ - B.8.b.6.0 to B.8.c.,0.9 - Road junction at B.7.c.,5.7½ - along North side of Road to Road Junction at A.12.c.,5.2 thence along West side of Road to Road Junction A.18.d.,3.8½ - thence along present boundary.

2. The new Sector will be occupied by the 118th Infantry Brigade 39th Division and the 234th Field Company R.E. 39th Division. The 39th Division are making arrangements for taking over the Sector in accordance with the attached March Table, and on completion of the relief the above troops will be attached to the 38th Division. The new Sector will form part of the front under the Command of the General Officer Commanding 38th Division.

3. After relief the Sector to be taken over will be known as the "LEFT SECTION", the present "LEFT SECTION" becoming the "CENTRE SECTION".

4. The 118th Infantry Brigade will be disposed as follows :-

   (a) Brigade H.Q. ELVERDINGHE CHATEAU.
   (b) 1 Battalion Front Line and Support.
       H.Q. BOESINGHE CHATEAU.
   (c) 1 Battalion in Reserve.
       H.Q. FERME DU BLEUET (B.10.c.,3.4)
   (d) 1 Battalion lent to the 114th Infantry Brigade to replace 10th Battalion The Welsh Regiment.
   (e) 1 Battalion in "L" Defences.
       H.Q. M.G.FARM.
       1 Company ELVERDINGHE.
       2 Companies L.8 (Garrison of L.10 to be found by these Companies)
       2 Platoons L.2.
       2 Platoons L.4
   (f) M.G.Company          ) In the area West of ELVER-
   (g) Stokes Mortar Battery) DINGHE now occupied by the *Rsve*
   (h) 1 Company R.E. (234th) Battalion 79th Regiment.
       Field Company R.E.)  ) Billets will be allotted by
                            ) 39th Division.

(i)

SECRET      MARCH TABLE (TO ACCOMPANY 38TH DIVISION ORDER NO. 71)

| Date | Unit | From | To | Remarks |
|---|---|---|---|---|
| Nov 28th | 1/1 Hertfordshire Regiment | Present billets | Camp "G" | For attachment to 38th Divn. in place of 10th Welsh Regt. |
| | 1/1 Cambridgeshire Regiment | -ditto- | Camp "J" | |
| | 1/5 Cheshire Regt. | -ditto- | POPERINGHE | |
| | 234th Field Coy. R.E. | -ditto- | Camp "F" | |
| | 118th M.G.Coy.} 118th T.M.Bty.} | -ditto- | Camp "F" | |
| Nov 29th | 118th Bde H.Q. 1/1 Cambridgeshire Regiment | Present billets Camp "J" | ELVERDINGHE ELVERDINGHE & "L" Defences. | Bn. of 55th Div. in "L" works will rejoin Division on relief French Battalion will move out of British area on relief. |
| | 1/6 Cheshire Regt. | POPERINGHE | Area immediately W. of ELVERDINGHE, now occupied by Bn. 79th Territorial Regt. "en repos". | |
| | 4/5 Black Watch 118th M.G.Coy. | Present billets Camp "F" | Camp "J" Trenches | Billeted in Reserve Area immediately W. of ELVERDINGHE |
| | 118th T.M.Bty. | Camp "F" | Reserve Area W. of ELVERDINGHE | |
| Nov 30th | DAY 4/5 Black Watch | Camp "J" | Relieves French Bn. in Support about FERME DO BLEUET | |
| | 234th Fd.Coy. R.E. | - | | Reconnoitres R.E. work in new Sector. |
| | NIGHT 1/6 Cheshire Regt. | Area W. of ELVERDINGHE | Front Line | French Bn. in front line moves out of British Area |
| Dec. 1st | 234th Field Coy. R.E. | Camp "F" | Reserve area W. of ELVERDINGHE | |

SECRET                   *War Diary*              COPY NO 27

*Appen 5.*

## 38TH (WELSH) DIVISION ORDER NO. 71

Reference :- 1/20,000 Map, Sheet 28 N.W.
and Trench Maps                     26th November 1916.

1. The Sector now held by the French 79th Territorial Regiment will be taken over by the VIII Corps on the 29th and 30th November 1916.
   This Sector extends from the present left of the 38th Division to B.6.c.,½.5 (trench A.6 inclusive).
   The Boundary between VIII Corps and Belgians will be :-

   B.6.c.,½.5 (junction of trenches A.6 and A.7) - BOYAU DE LA CHAPELLE (inclusive to VIII Corps) - Road at B.5.d.,7.1 - junction of trenches C.5 and C.6 at B.11.a.,7.7 - Road at B.11.a.,2.6½ - Cross Roads at B.10.b.,1.3½ - BOYAU DE BOESINGHE at B.9.b.,8.0 - Road at B.9.a.,2.3½ - B.8.b.,6.3½ - B.8.b.6.0 to B.8.c.,0.9 - Road junction at B.7.c.,5.7½ - along North side of Road to Road Junction at A.12.c.,5.2 thence along West side of Road to Road Junction A.18.d.,3.8½ - thence along present boundary.

2. The new Sector will be occupied by the 118th Infantry Brigade 39th Division and the 234th Field Company R.E. 39th Division. The 39th Division are making arrangements for taking over the Sector in accordance with the attached March Table, and on completion of the relief the above troops will be attached to the 38th Division. The new Sector will form part of the front under the Command of the General Officer Commanding 38th Division.

3. After relief the Sector to be taken over will be known as the "LEFT SECTION", the present "LEFT SECTION" becoming the "CENTRE SECTION".

4. The 118th Infantry Brigade will be disposed as follows :-

   (a) Brigade H.Q. ELVERDINGHE CHATEAU.
   (b) 1 Battalion Front Line and Support.
       H.Q. BOESINGHE CHATEAU.
   (c) 1 Battalion in Reserve.
       H.Q. FERME DU BLEUET (B.10.c.,3.4)
   (d) 1 Battalion lent to the 114th Infantry Brigade to replace 10th Battalion The Welsh Regiment.
   (e) 1 Battalion in "L" Defences.
       H.Q. M.G.FARM.
       1 Company ELVERDINGHE.
       2 Companies L.8 (Garrison of L.10 to be found by these Companies)
       2 Platoons L.2.
       2 Platoons L.4
   (f) M.G.Company           ) In the area West of ELVER-
   (g) Stokes Mortar Battery) DINGHE now occupied by the Rsve
   (h) 1 Company R.E. (234th) Battalion 79th Regiment.
       Field Company R.E.)     ) Billets will be allotted by
                                           ) 39th Division.

(i)

Page 2

       (i) Advanced Dressing Station.
           FERME 1889 (Road Junction B.9.c.,½.2½).
           Remainder of one Section Field Ambulance if
           required in the area West of ELVERDINGHE.

5. (a) General Officer Commanding 118th Infantry Brigade will take over Command of the Sector from COLONEL MORIN-PONS Commanding 79th French Regiment on completion of the relief on the night of November 30th/December 1st, and will then come under orders of the General Officer Commanding 38th Division.

   (b) The 1/1 Hertfordshire Regiment from "G" Camp will relieve the 17th Battalion Royal Welsh Fusiliers (lent to the 114th Infantry Brigade) in the Right Section on the 29th instant under orders of the General Officer Commanding 114th Infantry Brigade.
The 17th Battalion Royal Welsh Fusiliers 115th Infantry Brigade will move to "G" Camp on relief.

   (c) Machine Gun No. Z.1 will continue to be furnished by the Brigade in present Left Section for the present.

6. (a) The Group of Belgian Artillery at present covering the front of the new Sector will continue to do so under B.G.,R.A. 38th Division from 8 p.m. 30th instant until relieved by a portion of the 39th Divisional Artillery on the 8th/9th and 9th/10th December. The latter on completion of relief will come under the orders of the General Officer Commanding 38th Division. B.G's.R.A. 38th and 39th Division will arrange details of relief with the Commandant D'Artillerie, 5th Belgian Division.

   (b) The Trench Mortars of the 5th Belgian Division will remain in the Sector under orders of the General Officer Commanding 118th Infantry Brigade from 30th November until the Artillery relief is complete, and 2" Trench Mortars of the 39th Division have been installed. B.G., R.A. 38th Division will arrange for the ground to be reconnoitred, and positions suitable for our Trench Mortars selected.
These emplacements will be commenced as soon as the Infantry relief is complete.

7. A.D.A.S. VIII Corps is arranging to connect ELVERDINGHE CHATEAU with the existing buried cable system in the French area. The Signal system in the new Sector is being taken over by VIII Corps on the morning of November 30th. French Signallers will be left in Signal Stations with English Signallers until completion of relief on night November 30th/December 1st.
Officer Commanding 38th Divisional Signals will make himself acquainted with the Signal system, and arrange to co-ordinate it with the existing Divisional system. He will arrange for the Pigeon Stations with the Artillery to be relieved on 9th December.

8. C.E. VIII Corps is taking over R.E. work in the new Sector. C.R.E. 38th Division will communicate with COMMANDANT HUYGHE with reference to drainage and work in the new Sector.

9. The Railway line WOESTEN - ELVERDINGHE - ZUYDSCHOOTE will remain at the disposal of the 5th Belgian Divisional Artillery

10. Readjustment of Police Posts is being arranged by the A.P.M. VIII Corps.

11. Medical reliefs are being arranged between 79th French Regiment and 39th Division. The A.D.M.S. 38th Division will administer the medical arrangements in the new Sector on completion of relief.

12. The Officer Commanding Battalion at BOESINGHE CHATEAU will get in touch with Officer Commanding Right Battalion 5th Belgian Division at B.5.a.,4.2..
The liaison post at B.12.b.,5.5. will cease to be held on December 1st.
The cable to the latter will be continued to BOESINGHE CHATEAU.

13. Completion of relief will be reported to the 38th Division by code.

<u>A C K N O W L E D G E</u>

*[signature]*

Lieut. Colonel,
General Staff, 38th (Welsh) Divn.

26/11/1916.

Issued at :- 7 p.m.

Copies to :-

| | | |
|---|---|---|
| G.O.C. | 19th Welsh Regt. | VIII Corps |
| G.S. | A.D.M.S. | 55th Division |
| "Q" | Train | 5th Belgian Division |
| Signals | A.D.V.S. | 39th Division |
| C.R.A. | D.A.D.O.S. | R.T.O. POPERINGHE |
| C.R.E. | A.P.M. | Adj. i/c Camps |
| 113th Brigade | Camp Commdt. | 118th Brigade |
| 114th Brigade | Div. School | |
| 115th Brigade | 177th Tun:Coy. R.E. | |

S E C R E T   38th Division No. G.S.1149

| | |
|---|---|
| 113th Brigade | C. R. E. |
| 114th Brigade | 55th Division (For information) |
| 115th Brigade | 5th Belgian Div. ( " " ) |
| 38th Div. Arty. | 177th Tunnelling Coy. R.E. |
| | 19th Welsh Regt. |

The Signal for the withdrawal of the Raiding Party to-night will be given by one blast for ½ a minute on a Strombos Horn from TURCO FARM 35 minutes after Zero hour. All sentries will be warned that they are not to sound the Gas Alarm when it is heard.

In the event of the Strombos Horn failing French shunters horns will be blown by the Officers of the Raiding Party. The Signal for withdrawal will also be shown by the cessation of the Artillery barrage.

17/11/1916.

Lieut. Colonel,
General Staff, 38th (Welsh) Divn.

SECRET                                38th Division No. G.S.1149

```
113th Brigade      C. R. E.
114th Brigade      55th Division    (For information)
115th Brigade      5th Belgian Div. (    "        "   )
38th Div. Arty.    177th Tunnelling Coy. R.E.
                   19th Welsh Regt.
```

The Signal for the withdrawal of the Raiding Party to-night will be given by one blast for ½ a minute on a Strombos Horn from TURCO FARM 35 minutes after Zero hour. All sentries will be warned that they are not to sound the Gas Alarm when it is heard.

In the event of the Strombos Horn failing French shunters horns will be blown by the Officers of the Raiding Party. The Signal for withdrawal will also be shown by the cessation of the Artillery barrage.

17/11/1916.
                                        Lieut. Colonel,
                            General Staff, 38th (Welsh) Divn.

S E C R E T　　　　　　　　　　38th Division No. G.S.1149

113th Brigade　　　C. R. E.
114th Brigade　　　55th Division　(For information)
115th Brigade　　　5th Belgian Div. ("　　　　")
38th Div. Arty.　　177th Tunnelling Coy. R.E.
　　　　　　　　　19th Welsh Regt.

---

    The Signal for the withdrawal of the Raiding Party to-night will be given by one blast for ½ a minute on a Strombos Horn from TURCO FARM 35 minutes after Zero hour. All sentries will be warned that they are not to sound the Gas Alarm when it is heard.

    In the event of the Strombos Horn failing French shunters horns will be blown by the Officers of the Raiding Party. The Signal for withdrawal will also be shown by the cessation of the Artillery barrage.

*[signature]*
Lieut. Colonel,
17/11/1916.　　General Staff, 38th (Welsh) Divn.

13⎫
14⎬ Welsh
15⎭
114 M.G.Co.
114 T.M.B.
Brigade I.O.
Canal Bank Adjt. (for information)
Div Snipers

Please issue the necessary orders to all sentries.
　　　　　　　　　B.M.

38 DIV

**VERY SECRET.**

Copy No. 8

### 38TH (WELSH) DIVISION ORDER NO. 69.

15th November 1916.

1. A raid will be carried out by the 14th Battalion, Welsh Regiment on the night 17th/18th instant at a time and on an obective which have been communicated to the units concerned.

2. There will be no working or carrying parties North of CONEY STREET or East of BOUNDARY ROAD except such as General Officers Commanding 114th and 115th Brigades may order.

3. All horse transport must be West of the YPRES - ELVERDINGHE Road between 5-45.p.m. and 1.a.m. Motor lorries will be similarly restricted except those carrying the raiding party.

4. There will be no Buried Cable Working Party on the night 17th/18th instant.

PLEASE ACKNOWLEDGE

H.E. Pryce
Lieut. Colonel,
General Staff, 38th (Welsh) Division.

Issued to Signals at 6-30.p.m.

Copies to :-

| | | |
|---|---|---|
| G.O.C. | A.D.M.S. | VIII Corps |
| G.S. | Train | 55th Divn. |
| "Q" | A.D.V.S. | 5th Belgian Division. |
| Signals | D.A.D.O.S. | |
| C.R.A. | A.P.M. | |
| C.R.E. | Camp Comdt. | |
| 113th Bde. | Div: School | |
| 114th Bde. | 127th Tun.Coy. | |
| 115th Bde. | Corps O.P., No. 3. | |
| 19th Welsh Regt. | | |

SECRET
th Infantry Brigade.

SECRET.

To:-

Headquarters,

38th (Welsh) Division.

## Your G.S.1329.

Officer Commanding 13th Welsh has made out a plan for a raid on Sap 11, but it is dependent on firing two Bangalore Torpedoes in order to cut the wire and enter the Sap. The early hour of the bombardment on 28th instant precludes the laying of the Torpedoes, which is a lengthy proceeding. The raid cannot therefore be carried out in conjunction with the Trench Mortar bombardment. The latter is likely to put the Germans on the alert for a raid. The enemy are pretty sure to use a good many Very lights, which would also interfere with the enterprise.

I should prefer, therefore, to carry out the raid on another night, and this will be done unless orders to the contrary are received.

A patrol will be sent out tomorrow night at the time of the bombardment to ascertain the action of the enemy at Sap 11.

Brigadier General,
Commanding 114th Infantry Brigade.

G.O.C. 114th Infy Bde

The G.O.C. approves.

H.E. Pryce
Lt.Col
GS 38th Divn

27-11-16

SECRET

AMENDMENT TO 38TH (WELSH) DIVISION ORDER NO. 72.

30th November 1916.

1. Para. 2.   151st Field Company R.E. will proceed by lorry and not by train.

2. Para. 3.   19th (Pioneer) Battn. Welsh Regt. will be relieved on night 2nd/3rd December and not as previously stated.
An advance party of 13th (Pioneer) Battn. Gloucestershire Regt. will arrive at VLAMERTINGHE by lorry at midday 1st instant. Officer Commanding 19th (Pioneer) Battn. Welsh Regt will arrange to send a guide to meet them.
A guide should also be sent to report to Town Major, POPERINGHE at 8.a.m. 2nd instant to guide transport 13th Gloucestershire Regt. to HOPITAL FARM.

3. 19th (Pioneer) Battn. Welsh Regiment will report at HOULE on 4th December. Arrangements for the move will be issued by 38th Div: "Q".

Lieut. Colonel,
General Staff, 38th (Welsh) Division.

Copies issued as per Order No. 72.

*War Diary.*

SECRET

AMENDMENT TO 38TH (WELSH) DIVISION ORDER NO. 72.

30th November 1916.

1. Para. 2.    151st Field Company R.E. will proceed by lorry and not by train.

2. Para. 3.    19th (Pioneer) Battn. Welsh Regt. will be relieved on night 2nd/3rd December and not as previously stated.
An advance party of 13th (Pioneer) Battn. Gloucestershire Regt. will arrive at VLAMERTINGHE by lorry at midday 1st instant. Officer Commanding 19th (Pioneer) Battn. Welsh Regt will arrange to send a guide to meet them.
A guide should also be sent to report to Town Major, POPERINGHE at 8.a.m. 2nd instant to guide transport 13th Gloucestershire Regt. to HOPITAL FARM.

3. 19th (Pioneer) Battn. Welsh Regiment will report at HOULE on 4th December. Arrangements for the move will be issued by 38th Div: "Q".

Lieut. Colonel,
General Staff, 38th (Welsh) Division.

Copies issued as per Order No. 72.

S E C R E T                                     *Appen 6.*

COPY NO 37

## 38TH (WELSH) DIVISION ORDER NO. 72

Reference :- Map 1/20,000, Sheet 28 N.W.        30th November 1916.

1. The 151st Field Company R.E. and 19th (Pioneer) Battn. Welsh Regiment will move by rail to HOULE to construct rifle ranges under the supervision of the C.R.E. 39th Division.

2. The 225th Field Company R.E. will relieve the 151st Field Company R.E. on the night 1st/2nd December. The latter (less one Section) will entrain at POPERINGHE on the 2nd December at 8.30 a.m.
One Section 151st Field Company R.E. will proceed to HOULE to-morrow (December 1st) by lorries from 151st Field Company Transport Line at 8.30 a.m.

3. The 15th (Pioneer) Battalion Gloucester Regiment will relieve the 19th (Pioneer) Battalion Welsh Regiment on night December 1st/2nd. The latter will assemble at Camp "J" in readiness to entrain at short notice.

4. Details of relief will be arranged between Officers Commanding Units concerned. Details of work, copies of the Defence Scheme, Trench Stores will be handed over by the outgoing to the incoming Units.

5. No formed bodies will move East of the VLAMERTINGHE - ELVERDINGHE ROAD before 4.15 p.m.

6. Orders for the move by rail and lorries will be issued by "Q" 38th Division.

7. The 225th Field Company R.E. and 13th (Pioneer) Battn. Gloucester Regiment will come under the orders of the General Officer Commanding 38th Division on completion of moves.

8. Completion of relief will be reported by Code.

*Acknowledge.*                     *A Derry Mayrfor*

Lieut. Colonel,
General Staff, 38th (Welsh) Divn.

Issued to Signals at 4.30 p.m.
Copies to :-

| | | |
|---|---|---|
| G.O.C. | 19th Welsh Regt. | VIII Corps |
| G.S. | A.D.M.S. | 55th Division |
| "Q" | Train | 39th Division |
| Signals | A.D.V.S. | R.T.O. POPERINGHE |
| C.R.A. | D.A.D.O.S. | 5th Belgian Divn. |
| C.R.E. | A.P.M. | Adj. i/c Camps |
| 113th Brigade | Camp Commdt. | |
| 114th Brigade | Div. School | |
| 115th Brigade | 177th Tun:Coy. R.E. | |

SECRET  *War Diary Appen 6.*

COPY NO. 26

## 38TH (WELSH) DIVISION ORDER NO. 72

Reference :- Map 1/20,000, Sheet 28 N.W.     30th November 1916.

1. The 151st Field Company R.E. and 19th (Pioneer) Battn. Welsh Regiment will move by rail to HOULE to construct rifle ranges under the supervision of the C.R.E. 39th Division.

2. The 225th Field Company R.E. will relieve the 151st Field Company R.E. on the night 1st/2nd December. The latter (less one Section) will entrain at POPERINGHE on the 2nd December at 8.30 a.m.
One Section 151st Field Company R.E. will proceed to HOULE to-morrow (December 1st) by lorries from 151st Field Company Transport Line at 8.30 a.m.

3. The 15th (Pioneer) Battalion Gloucester Regiment will relieve the 19th (Pioneer) Battalion Welsh Regiment on night December 1st/2nd. The latter will assemble at Camp "J" in readiness to entrain at short notice.

4. Details of relief will be arranged between Officers Commanding Units concerned. Details of work, copies of the Defence Scheme, Trench Stores will be handed over by the outgoing to the incoming Units.

5. No formed bodies will move East of the VLAMERTINGHE - ELVERDINGHE ROAD before 4.15 p.m.

6. Orders for the move by rail and lorries will be issued by "Q" 38th Division.

7. The 225th Field Company R.E. and 13th (Pioneer) Battn. Gloucester Regiment will come under the orders of the General Officer Commanding 38th Division on completion of moves.

8. Completion of relief will be reported by Code.

*Acknowledge*

*A Derry Mayntor*
Lieut. Colonel,
General Staff, 38th (Welsh) Divn.

Issued to Signals at 4.30 p.m.
Copies to :-

| | | |
|---|---|---|
| G.O.C. | 19th Welsh Regt. | VIII Corps |
| G.S. | A.D.M.S. | 55th Division |
| "Q" | Train | 39th Division |
| Signals | A.D.V.S. | R.T.O. POPERINGHE |
| C.R.A. | D.A.D.O.S. | 5th Belgian Divn. |
| C.R.E. | A.P.M. | Adj. i/c Camps |
| 113th Brigade | Camp Commdt. | |
| 114th Brigade | Div. School | |
| 115th Brigade | 177th Tun:Coy. R.E. | |

SECRET      MARCH TABLE (TO ACCOMPANY 38TH DIVISION ORDER NO. 71)

| Date | Unit | From | To | Remarks |
|---|---|---|---|---|
| Nov 28th | 1/1 Hertfordshire Regiment | Present billets | Camp "G" | For attachment to 38th Divn. in place of 10th Welsh Regt. |
|  | 1/1 Cambridgeshire Regiment | -ditto- | Camp "J" |  |
|  | 1/6 Cheshire Regt. | -ditto- | POPERINGHE |  |
|  | 234th Field Coy. R.E. | -ditto- | Camp "F" |  |
|  | 118th M.G.Coy. ) 118th T.M.Bty. ) | -ditto- | Camp "F" |  |
| Nov 29th | 118th Bde H.Q. 1/1 Cambridgeshire Regiment, 1/6 Cheshire Regt. | Present billets Camp "J" POPERINGHE | ELVERDINGHE ELVERDINGHE & "L" Defences. Area immediately W. of ELVERDINGHE, now occupied by Bn. 79th.Territorial Rgt. "en repos". | Bn. of 55th Div. in "L" works will rejoin Division on relief French Battalion will move out of British area on relief. |
|  | 4/5 Black Watch 118th M.G.Coy. | Present billets Camp "F" | Camp "J" | Billeted in Reserve Area immediately W. of ELVERDINGHE |
|  | 118th T.M.Bty. | Camp "F" | Trenches |  |
| Nov 30th | DAY 4/5 Black Watch | Camp "J" | Reserve Area W. of ELVERDINGHE |  |
|  | 234th Fd.Coy. R.E. | — | Relieves French Bn. in Support about FERME DO BLEUET |  |
|  | NIGHT 1/6 Cheshire Regt. | Area W. of ELVERDINGHE | Front Line |  |
| Dec. 1st | 234th Field Coy. R.E. | Camp "F" | Reserve area W. of ELVERDINGHE | Reconnoitres R.E. work in new Sector. French Bn. in front line moves out of British Area |

Page 3

9. The Railway line WOESTEN - ELVERDINGHE - ZUYDSCHOOTE will remain at the disposal of the 5th Belgian Divisional Artillery

10. Readjustment of Police Posts is being arranged by the A.P.M. VIII Corps.

11. Medical reliefs are being arranged between 79th French Regiment and 39th Division. The A.D.M.S. 38th Division will administer the medical arrangements in the new Sector on completion of relief.

12. The Officer Commanding Battalion at BOESINGHE CHATEAU will get in touch with Officer Commanding Right Battalion 5th Belgian Division at B.5.a.,4.2..
The liaison post at B.12.b.,5.5. will cease to be held on December 1st.
The cable to the latter will be continued to BOESINGHE CHATEAU.

13. Completion of relief will be reported to the 38th Division by code.

A C K N O W L E D G E

*[signature]*

Lieut. Colonel,
General Staff, 38th (Welsh) Divn.

26/11/1916.

Issued at :- 7 p.m.

Copies to :-

| | | |
|---|---|---|
| G.O.C. | 19th Welsh Regt. | VIII Corps |
| G.S. | A.D.M.S. | 55th Division |
| "Q" | Train | 5th Belgian Division |
| Signals | A.D.V.S. | 39th Division |
| C.R.A. | D.A.D.O.S. | R.T.O. POPERINGHE |
| C.R.E. | A.P.M. | Adj. i/c Camps |
| 113th Brigade | Camp Commdt. | 118th Brigade |
| 114th Brigade | Div. School | |
| 115th Brigade | 177th Tun:Coy. R.E. | |

(i) Advanced Dressing Station.
   FERME 1889 (Road Junction B.9.c.,$\frac{1}{2}$.2$\frac{1}{2}$).
   Remainder of one Section Field Ambulance if
   required in the area West of ELVERDINGHE.

5. (a)
   General Officer Commanding 118th Infantry Brigade will
   take over Command of the Sector from COLONEL MORIN-PONS
   Commanding 79th French Regiment on completion of the
   relief on the night of November 30th/December 1st, and
   will then come under orders of the General Officer
   Commanding 38th Division.
   (b)
   The 1/1 Hertfordshire Regiment from "G" Camp will relieve
   the 17th Battalion Royal Welsh Fusiliers (lent to the
   114th Infantry Brigade) in the Right Section on the 29th
   instant under orders of the General Officer Commanding
   114th Infantry Brigade.
   The 17th Battalion Royal Welsh Fusiliers 115th Infantry
   Brigade will move to "G" Camp on relief.
   (c)
   Machine Gun No. Z.1 will continue to be furnished by the
   Brigade in present Left Section for the present.

6. (a)
   The Group of Belgian Artillery at present covering the
   front of the new Sector will continue to do so under
   B.G.,R.A. 38th Division from 8 p.m. 30th instant until
   relieved by a portion of the 39th Divisional Artillery
   on the 8th/9th and 9th/10th December. The latter on
   completion of relief will come under the orders of the
   General Officer Commanding 38th Division. B.G's.R.A.
   38th and 39th Division will arrange details of relief
   with the Commandant D'Artillerie, *5th Belgian Division*.
   (b)
   The Trench Mortars of the 5th Belgian Division will
   remain in the Sector under orders of the General Officer
   Commanding 118th Infantry Brigade from 30th November
   until the Artillery relief is complete, and 2" Trench
   Mortars of the 39th Division have been installed. B.G.,
   R.A. 38th Division will arrange for the ground to be
   reconnoitred, and positions suitable for our Trench
   Mortars selected.
   These emplacements will be commenced as soon as the
   Infantry relief is complete.

7. A.D.A.S. VIII Corps is arranging to connect ELVERDINGHE
   CHATEAU with the existing buried cable system in the
   French area. The Signal system in the new Sector is
   being taken over by VIII Corps on the morning of November
   30th. French Signallers will be left in Signal Stations
   with English Signallers until completion of relief on
   night November 30th/December 1st.
   Officer Commanding 38th Divisional Signals will make
   himself acquainted with the Signal system, and arrange
   to co-ordinate it with the existing Divisional system.
   He will arrange for the Pigeon Stations with the Artillery
   to be relieved on 9th December.

8. C.E. VIII Corps is taking over R.E. work in the new
   Sector.  C.R.E. 38th Division will communicate with
   COMMANDANT HUYGHE with reference to drainage and work in
   the new Sector.

9.

# WAR DIARY
## INTELLIGENCE SUMMARY

Army Form C. 2118.

Original
Volume XIII

| Place | Date | Hour | Summary of Events and Information | Remarks and references to Appendices |
|---|---|---|---|---|
| ST SIXTE | December 1916 | | | |
| | 1st. | | 118th Brigade, 39th Division took over BOESINGHE SECTOR. ESSEX TRENCH raided by the enemy, under cover of intense Trench Mortar and Artillery fire. 16th Royal Welsh Fusiliers holding the trench suffered some casualties. There was a Conference at VIII Corps Headquarters in the afternoon. Operation Order No.73 issued. | GDB Apx I when it was inspected by G.O.C. |
| | 2nd. | | 19th Pioneer Battalion, Welsh Regt moved to J Camp from CANAL BANK. Situation normal. | GDB |
| | 3rd. | | Hostile artillery active against Left and Centre Brigades. Situation normal. Col. Lieut.Colonel.H.E.PRYCE removed to No.46 Casualty Clearing Station, sick. | GDB |
| | 4th. | | General Officer Commanding met Brig-General E.H.FINCH HATTON, Commanding, 118th Brigade, and visited the BOESINGHE SECTOR. Night 4/5th December 115th Brigade relieved 114th Brigade in the Right Sector. Situation normal. Slight shelling of the CANAL BANK by the enemy. | GDB |
| | 5th. | | General Officer Commanding visited the trenches in the LANCASHIRE FARM and BOESINGHE SECTORS. Some hostile artillery activity against WHITE TRENCH, NILE and LANCASHIRE FARM. | GDB |
| | 6th. | | Slight hostile artillery activity in the neighbourhood of ESSEX TRENCH and CLIFFORD TOWERS. General Officer Commanding visited 15th Welsh Regt. in the morning. | GDB |
| | 7th. | | Situation normal. | GDB Apx II |
| | 8th. | | Situation normal. The 2nd Army Commander, Lieut.General, Sir H.PLUMER, inspected the 38th Divisional School. Operation Order No.74 issued. | GDB |
| | 9th. | | Some hostile artillery activity reported near the NILE. Operation Order No.74 issued. | GDB |
| | 10th. | | The Stokes Mortars of 113th Brigade bombarded CAESARS NOSE with effect. | GDB |
| | 11th. | | Hostile Field Artillery active against the left Sector. Situation normal. Relief of General Officer Commanding visited 38th Divisional School. | GDB |
| | 12th. | | 38th(Welsh) Division by 39th Division commenced. | GDB |
| | 13th. | | General Officer Commanding and Major A.DERRY (Brigade Major, 115th Brigade and acting G.S.O.1) attended a Conference at VIII Corps Headquarters. Situation normal. All documents relating to Divisional Area handed over to 39th Division. G.S.O.2. CAPTAIN. A.F.SMITH, M.C. COLDSTREAM GUARDS, returned from a course for Senior Staff Officers at G.H.Q. Situation normal. Relief of 118th Brigade by 115th Brigade completed. | GDB |
| | 14th. | 11.a.m | General Officer Commanding, 39th Division, Major General, C.J.CUTHBERT, C.B., C.M.G. took over command of the left Sector of the VIII Corps front at ST SIXTE. 38th Divisional Headquarters opened at ESQUELBECQ the same hour. | GDB |
| ESQUELBECQ. | 15th. | | Units of the Division engaged in training in the Reserve Area. | |
| | | | Units | |

# WAR DIARY

**Army Form C. 2118.**

Instructions regarding War Diaries and Intelligence Summaries are contained in F. S. Regs, Part II. and the Staff Manual respectively. Title Pages will be prepared in manuscript.

| Place | Date | Hour | Summary of Events and Information | Remarks and references to Appendices |
|---|---|---|---|---|
| ESQUELBECQ. | 16th. | | Units of the Division engaged in training. Relief of 38th Divisional Artillery by 39th Divisional Artillery complete. The whole Division(less 115th Brigade and 123rd Field Coy. Royal Engineers still attached to 39th Division) is now in the VIII Corps Reserve Area, and distributed according to the location list in Appendix. Conference at VIII Corps Headquarters. Units training. | GDB Appx II GDB GDC |
| | 17th. | | | |
| | 18th. | | | |
| | 19th. | | The Commander-in-Chief, General Sir D. HAIG, inspected the 113th Brigade at BOLLEZEELE, and the 121st Brigade, Royal Field Artillery at WATOU. 119th Brigade Royal Field Artillery moved by road to WISSANT for training purposes. General Officer Commanding indisposed, and unable to attend inspection by the Commander-in-Chief. G.S.O.2., A.A.&Q.M.G. attended and were presented to the Commander-in-Chief. Operation Order No.75 issued. | Appx III GDB GDB |
| | 20th. | | Units training. | |
| | 21st. | | Units training. | |
| | 22nd. | | The enemy raided the trenches occupied by 17th Royal Welsh Fusiliers in the BOESINGHE SECTOR. Two Lewis Guns and 14th other ranks reported missing. Units training. | GDB GDB |
| | 23rd. | | General Officer Commanding inspected the 38th Divisional Signal School at KIEKEN PUT. Units training. 10th South Wales Borderers arrived at 2nd Army School of Instruction. | GDB |
| | 24th. | | Instructions received from VIII Corps for removal of 38th Divisional School to Camp.J. 124th Field Company, Royal Engineers moved to WATTEN from MEROKEGHEM for technical training. Operation Order No.76 issued. Units training. | GDB |
| | 25th. | | | |
| | 26th. | | General Officer Commanding visited HOUILLE, WATTEN and TILQUES, inspecting 11th South Wales Borderers, 124th Field Company, Royal Engineers, and 13th Welsh Regt. Units training. Operation Order No.76 cancelled. | GDB |
| | 27th. | | Units training. Conference at VIII Corps Headquarters. G.S.O.2. attended. | |
| | 28th. | | General Officer Commanding proceeded on 4 days leave to PARIS. Brigadier-General T.O. MARDEN assumed temporary command of the Division in his absence. Units training. Operation Order No.77 issued. 121 Bde R.F.A left for WISSANT to relieve 119 Bde R.F.A. | Appx IV GDB GDB |
| | 29th. | | Units training. 123 Bde R.F.A. left for WISSANT to relieve 119 Bde R.F.A. | |
| | 30th. | | 38th Divisional school moved to Camp.J. Units training. Relief of 115th Brigade in BOESINGHE SECTOR by 116th Brigade. | |
| | 31st. | | Moves in accordance with Operation Order No.77 complete. | |

Drake Brockman
Capt. G.S.
38th Division

1-12-1916

War Diary app. I
COPY NO 26

SECRET

## 38TH (WELSH) DIVISION ORDER NO.73

Reference :- Map 1/20,000, Sheet 28 N.W.    1st December 1916

1. On the night of 4th/5th December the 115th Infantry Brigade (less one Battalion) will relieve the 114th Infantry Brigade in the Right Section.
The Battalion of the 115th Infantry Brigade remaining in the Reserve Brigade Area will be accommodated in "G" Camp, and will be under the orders of the General Officer Commanding 114th Infantry Brigade.

2. The 114th Infantry Brigade will place one Battalion at the disposal of the General Officer Commanding 115th Infantry Brigade until the 9th December. On the night December 9/10 the Battalion will be relieved by the Battalion of the 115th Infantry Brigade in "G" Camp.

3. All details of relief will be arranged between the Brigadiers concerned.

4. No formed bodies of the 115th Infantry Brigade will be East of the VLAMERTINGHE - ELVERDINGHE ROAD before 4.15 p.m.

5. The General Officer Commanding 115th Infantry Brigade will assume command of the Right Section on completion of relief which will be reported to Divisional Headquarters.

6. The Platoon of the 115th Infantry Brigade at the Divisional School will rejoin its Brigade at 2 p.m. on the 4th December. The General Officer Commanding 114th Infantry Brigade will detail one Platoon to proceed to "H" Camp on the morning of December 5th where it will come under the orders of the Commandant Divisional School.

7. On the nights of 4th/5th December and 5th/6th December there will be no Cable Burying, and on the 4th and 5th December no work on Horse Standings.
The 114th Infantry Brigade will start work on Horse Standings on December 6th, and will find Cable Burying parties on and after 6th December.

ACKNOWLEDGE

Lieut. Colonel,
General Staff, 38th (Welsh) Division.

Issued to Signals at 6.30 p.m.
Copies to :-

| | | |
|---|---|---|
| G.O.C. | 19th Welsh Regt. | 177th Tun: Coy. R.E. |
| G.S. | A.D.M.S. | 55th Division |
| "Q" | Train | 39th Division |
| Signals | S.S.O. | 5th Belgian Division. |
| C.R.A. | A.D.V.S. | R.T.O. POPERINGHE |
| C.R.E. | D.A.D.O.S. | Adj. i/c Camps. |
| 113th Brigade | A.P.M. | 118th Brigade |
| 114th Brigade | Camp Comdt. | |
| 115th Brigade | Div. School | |

*app: II*

S E C R E T                                         Copy No. 34

## 38TH (WELSH) DIVISION ORDER NO. 74.

Reference :- Maps Sheets 27 & 28 1/40,000      9th December 1916.

1.  (a) 39th Division will relieve 38th Division in the Left Sector. The relief will commence on December 11th and be completed by December 14th in accordance with the attached Movement Table.

    (b) 113th Infantry Brigade will move to BOLLEZEELE Area.
    114th Infantry Brigade will move to K.L.M.N.Y.Z. Camps.
    115th Infantry Brigade and 123rd Field Coy.R.E. will be attached to 39th Division and will take over Left Section, and "L" Works.

    (c) 1/1st Herts. Regt. (attached to 114th Bde.) will move under orders of G.O.C., 39th Division.

    (d) 115th Infantry Brigade will hold a Battalion in readiness to proceed to Second Army School about 18th December.
    114th Infantry Brigade will hold a battalion in readiness to proceed to HOULE about 14th December.

2.  Details of relief will be arranged direct between the Brigadiers concerned.

3.  Machine Gun Companies and Light Trench Mortar Batteries will carry out reliefs as far as possible in daylight. In any case they will be completed so as not to interfere with Infantry reliefs.

4.  Statements of work in progress, aeroplane photographs, trench maps and copies of Brigade and Battalion Defence Schemes, trench stores and Reserve Ammunition will be handed over and receipts obtained.

5.  No formed bodies will move East of ELVERDINGHE - VLAMERTINGHE road before 4-15.p.m. When relieving in the Left Section, communication trenches and not roads will be used by parties of men however small during daylight.

6.  Artillery reliefs will be carried out after the completion of Infantry reliefs, commencing on 14th December under instructions to be issued by G.O.C., R.A., VIII Corps.

7.  R.E. reliefs will be arranged direct between C.R.E's. The scheme of work showing the work in hand and work proposed will be handed over.

8.  R.A.M.C. reliefs and Sanitary Section will be carried out between A.D.M.S. of Divisions under instructions of D.D.M.S. VIII Corps.

9.  Mobile Vet. Section will be relieved by Mobile Vet. Section, 39th Division under arrangements to be made by Officers Commanding Units concerned.

10. D.A.D.O.S. will arrange to take over from D.A.D.O.S., 39th Division under orders to be issued by 38th Div: "Q".

11. Divisional Schools, Sniping School and Gas School will remain in their present locations.

12. Divisional Train will move under orders to be issued by 38th Div: "Q".

13. Arrangements for billeting and entraining will be made by "Q".

14. Divisional H.Q. will close at ST.SIXTE at 11.a.m. on 14th instant and open at the same hour at ESQUELBECQ. At this hour G.O.C., 39th Division will assume command of the Left Division Area.

15. Completion of reliefs will be reported to Divisional H.Q..

A C K N O W L E D G E.

Major for Lieut. Colonel,
General Staff, 38th (Welsh) Division.

Issued to Signals at 12 noon.

Copies to :-

| | | |
|---|---|---|
| G.O.C. | 19th Welsh Regt. | Gas Officer. |
| G.S. | A.D.M.S. | Sniping Coy. |
| "Q" | Train | 13th Gloucesters. |
| Signals | S.S.O. | 118th Brigade |
| C.R.A. | A.D.V.S. | 177th Tun.Coy.,R.E. |
| C.R.E. | D.A.D.O.S. | VIII Corps |
| 113th Brigade | A.P.M. | 39th Division |
| 114th Brigade | Camp Comdt. | 55th Division |
| 115th Brigade | Div: School. | 5th Belgian Division |
| | | R.T.O. POP. |
| | | D.A.D.P.S., VIII Corps. |
| | | Adjt. i/c Camps. |

S E C R E T      MOVE TABLE (TO ACCOMPANY 38TH (WELSH) DIVISION ORDER NO. 74)

| Date | Unit | From | To | Relieving Units of | Relieved by Units of | Remarks |
|---|---|---|---|---|---|---|
| Decr. 11th | 114th Bde (less 10th Bn. Welsh Regt. and 1/1st Herts Regt) | D.E.G.P.S Camps | K.L.M.N.Y.Z. Camps | 116th Bde. | 115th Bde. | March route. 114th Bde. move by day. |
| Decr.11th/12th. | 2 Bns. 115th Brigade 115th M.G.Coy. and L.T.M.Bty. 123rd Fd.Coy.R.E. | Support Right Sec) Right Section ) ) | D.E.G.P.S. Camps Loft Section | 114th Bde. 234th Fd.Coy. R.E. | 116th Bde. One Fd.Coy. 39th Divn. | By train March route |
| Decr.12th/13th. | 2 Bns. 113th Brigade 2 Bns. 115th Bdo. 115th M.G.Coy. and L.T.M.Bty. 115th Bde.(less two Bns.) 115th M.G.Coy and L.T.M.Battery | Support Centre Sec D.E.G.P.S. Camps Front Line Right Section | POPERINGHE Left Section D.E.G.P.S. Camps | — 118th .do. 115th Bde. | 117th Bde. 115th .de. 116th .de. | By train March route March route |
| Decr. 13th | H.Q. 115th Brigade | Camp D. | ELVERDINGHE | 118th Bde. | — | March route |
| Decr. 13th/14th. | 2 Bns. 115th Brigade | D.E.G.P.S. Camps | ELVERDINGHE, "L" Line and area West of ELVERDINGHE | 118th Bde. | — | March route |
| | 2 Bns. 113th Brigade | POPERINGHE | BOLLEZEELE Area | 117th Bde. | 117th Bde. | By train |
| | 113th Brigade (less 2 Battalions | Front Line, Centre Section. | POPERINGHE | 113th Bde. | 117th Bde. | |
| Decr. 14th | 38th Division H.Q. 113th Brigade (less two Battalions). | ST. SIXTE POPERINGHE | ESQUELBECQ BOLLEZEELE Area | H.Q. 39th Div 117th Brigade | — | By train |

9/12/1916.

G.P.L.Drake-Brockman
Major for Capt
for Lieut. Colonel,
General Staff, 38th (Welsh) Division.

Index

# SUBJECT.

| No. | Contents. | Date. |
|---|---|---|
| | 38th DIVISION<br><br>**IMPORTANT**<br><br>NOT TO BE SHOWN TO VISITORS. | |

P.A. in 38th Division

G.S.

December 1915.


NOT TO BE AVAILABLE FOR

VISITORS.

C.2 Precis Report No. 117, page 3, No. 1115.

Referring Files O.B./A.2360; A.G/A.17748; M.S. 19318.

## 38th Division.

1115 SECRET.   Training of 38th Division - December 1915 and September 1916.

On 1/12/15 the W.O. say that the 38th (Welsh) Division is a little behind other Divisions recently sent to France in the matter of efficiency; it is understood the conditions at the front will admit of further training being given without inconvenience.

There is a D.O. letter from General Paget to the same effect. The Division was originally raised by Mr. Lloyd George "As a consequence, practically all the Brigade Commanders and Commanders of Battalions, as well as many of the officers had to be changed. The original men were either civilians or aged dug-outs".

In reply to the W.O. the C-in-C. points out that the division is to replace well-trained troops sent from France, and urges the necessity of training in France being reduced to a minimum.

In Sept. 1916, Gen. Plumer in a D.O. says he is not satisfied with the 38th Division. There is a lack of enterprise and real discipline; an infusion of new blood is wanted. The Welsh Division being the creation of Mr. Lloyd George makes the situation a little difficult.

G.H.Q. think it a pity to try and bolster up a Welsh Divn. with good officers and N.C.O's from English formations. No Divisions are so well placed as to be able to spare their best to make up deficiencies in an inferior division. The A.G. is said to be dealing with Gen. Plumer's official report; the latter is not in the file.

~~S. SECRET~~

(6359) Wt. W160/M3016 1,500,000 10/17 McA & W Ltd (E 1898) Forms W3091.    Army Form W.3091.

~~SS143~~/E    **Cover for Documents.**

**Nature of Enclosures.**

~~38th Divn: Orders & Instrns~~

**Notes, or Letters written.**

Vol. 14.

General Staff,
38th Division.

January 1917

# WAR DIARY of General Staff, 38th (Welsh) Divn

**Army Form C. 2118.**

## INTELLIGENCE SUMMARY

*(Erase heading not required.)*

1st January 1917.

Volume XIV

Original

J.E./14

| Place | Date 1917 | Hour | Summary of Events and Information | Remarks and references to Appendices |
|---|---|---|---|---|
| ESQUELBECQ | 1/1/17 | | 38th Division in Corps Reserve. Units training. | GDB |
| " | 2/1/17 | | 38th Division in Corps Reserve. Units training. | GDB |
| " | 3/1/17 | | 38th Division in Corps Reserve. Units training. | GDB |
| " | 4/1/17 | | 38th Division in Corps Reserve. Units training. | GDB |
| " | 5/1/17 | | G.O.C. 38th Division and Lieut. General SIR H.PLUMER Commanding Second Army inspected the 115th Brigade. Units training. | GDB |
| " | 6/1/17 | | G.S.O. II Captain A.F.SMITH, M.C. proceeded to CHATEAU LOVIE, VIII Corps H.Q. to arrange details of relief of 39th Division by 38th Division. | GDB |
| " | 7/1/17 | | Units training. | GDB |
| " | 8/1/17 | | G.O.C. visited the 115th Brigade at BOLLEZEELE. Conference at VIII Corps H.Q. in the afternoon. G.O.C.; G.S.O.II (Captain A.F.SMITH, M.C.), A.A. & Q.M.G., C.R.A. and C.R.E. attended. O.O. No.78 issued. | GDB Appx. I |
| " | 9/1/17 | | Units training. | GDB |
| " | 10/1/17 | | 121st Brigade R.F.A. started to march from WISSANT to rejoin the Division. O.O. 79 issued. | Appx. II |
| " | 11/1/17 | | G.O.C. and G.S.O.II visited the forward area. | GDB |
| " | 12/1/17 | | G.O.C. and G.S.O.II visited the Second Army School at WISQUES and 11th South Wales Borderers at TATINGHEM. Conference at Divisional H.Q. 5.15 p.m. G.O.C., G.O's.C. 113th, 114th and 115th Brigades, C.R.A. and C.R.E. present. | GDB |
| " | 13/1/17 | | Relief of 39th Division by 38th Division commenced in accordance with O.O's. 78 and 79. | GDB |
| " | 14/1/17 | | G.O.C. and G.S.O.II visited VIII Corps H.Q. and Headquarters 39th Division. | GDB |
| " and ST.SIXTE | 15/1/17 | | G.S.O.II visited Headquarters 55th Division. H.Q. 38th Division closed at ESQUELBECQ and opened at ST. SIXTE 10 a.m. Enemy shelled "X" Line heavily during the evening causing some casualties. Considerable hostile artillery activity in the region of WIELTJE. | GDB |
| " | 16/1/17 | | Conference at VIII Corps H.Q. 3 p.m. G.O.C. and G.S.O.II attended. Situation normal. | GDB |
| " | 17/1/17 | | G.O.C. and G.S.O.II visited the trenches in the left (BOESINGHE) Section. Situation quiet. | GDB |
| " | 18/1/17 | | G.O.C. and G.S.O.II visited the trenches of the Right Section. Slight hostile shelling of BILGE TRENCH. Relief of 39th Division by 38th Division complete, and Units billeted in accordance with Appendix . 164th Brigade 55th Division, and 2/1st W.Lancs.Coy. R.E. attached, also 196th Machine Gun Company. | GDB Appx. III |
| " | 19/1/17 | | Hostile Artillery very active against the trenches of the Centre Section. | GDB |
| " | 20/1/17 | | Hostile Artillery very active during the day in all three Brigade Areas. | GDB |

Army Form C. 2118.

# WAR DIARY
## or
## INTELLIGENCE SUMMARY

(Erase heading not required.)

Instructions regarding War Diaries and Intelligence Summaries are contained in F. S. Regs., Part II. and the Staff Manual respectively. Title Pages will be prepared in manuscript.

| Place | Date | Hour | Summary of Events and Information | Remarks and references to Appendices |
|---|---|---|---|---|
| ST. SIXTE | 21/1/17. | | O.O. No. 80 issued. Hostile Artillery active on Left Brigade front. | |
| " | 22/1/17. | | Hostile Trench Mortars active against the Left Brigade. | |
| " | 23/1/17. | | G.O.C. and G.S.O.III visited the "X" Line in the Left Brigade. Hostile Artillery and trench mortars very active against BOESINGHE during the morning. | |
| " | 24/1/17. | | Considerable aerial activity throughout the day. Brigadier General E.L.ELLINGTON G.S.VIII Corps visited 38th Divisional H.Q. G.S.O.II visited Headquarters, VIII Corps. Hostile Artillery shelled the left and centre brigade during the day. | |
| " | 25/1/17. | | Corps Conference at 3 p.m. G.O.C. and G.S.O.11 attended. Situation normal. Corps Commander VIII Corps Sir A. HUNTER-WESTON K.C.B., D.S.O. visited Headquarters 38th Division and explained | |
| " | 26/1/17. | | Corps Commander VIII Corps Sir A.HUNTER WESTON, K.C.B., D.S.O. visited Headquarters 38th Division and explained that there were possibilities of a hostile attack. Certain precautions taken. Slight hostile artillery activity during the day. In the evening there was a test alarm for manning the "L" Line. | |
| " | 27/1/17. | | Intermittent hostile shelling during the day. | |
| " | 28/1/17. | | Slight hostile artillery activity. | |
| " | 29/1/17. | | The Army Commander Sir H.PLUMER visited the G.O.C. Our Artillery active during the afternoon. | |
| " | 30/1/17. | | Our Artillery assisted the Belgians to repel a raid in the vicinity of HETSAS. Hostile Arty. active during the right 30/31st against the Centre Brigade especially against TURCO FARM AREA. | |
| " | 31/1/17. | | G.O.C. visited 164th Brigade at Camp "D" Hostile Artillery active against the Centre Brigade. | |

6/2/1917.

E.P. Drake-Brockman Capt.
for
Major General,
Commanding 38th (Welsh) Division.

Secret

Vol 15

"War Diary of General
Staff 38th (Welsh) Division

Volume XV

February 1917

Army Form C. 2118

# WAR DIARY OF 38TH (WELSH) DIVISION.

## INTELLIGENCE SUMMARY

VOLUME XV.

Instructions regarding War Diaries and Intelligence Summaries are contained in F. S. Regs., Part II. and the Staff Manual respectively. Title Pages will be prepared in manuscript.

| Place | Date | Hour | Summary of Events and Information | Remarks and references to Appendices |
|---|---|---|---|---|
| ST SIXTE. | FEBRUARY. 1st. | | Bombardment of enemy Lines in C.7 by Heavy Artillery, Field Artillery, Medium and Stokes T.M's. Enemy retaliation on BOESINGHE Section was ineffective. | |
| | 2nd. | | Enemy bombarded front line in BOESINGHE section with Minenwerfer, and VILLAGE, Support Line, and Communication Trenches with Artillery in the early morning and at intervals during the day. Our Artillery retaliated vigorously. | |
| | 3rd. | | Slight enemy artillery activity against HUDDERSFIELD and CANAL BANK. | |
| | 4th. | | Quiet day. | |
| | 5th. | | Enemy aeroplane dropped bombs on PROVEN. | |
| | 6th. | | Heavy and Divisional Artillery, also Medium and Stokes Trench Mortars, bombarded KRUPP SALIENT. Slight enemy retaliation on RAMGATE, SKIPTON, LANCASHIRE FARM and CANAL BANK. | |
| | 7th. | | Hostile artillery activity against ELVERDINGHE and ROUSSEL FARM. Enemy T.M's on LANCASHIRE FARM and EALING. | |
| | 8th. | | Heavy enemy shelling of DECOUCK FARM and Battery positions near ELVERDINGHE. 115th Brigade Machine Gun Company and 115th Brigade Trench Mortar Battery moved headquarters from DE COUCK FARM to EMILE FARM. G.O.C. at Corps Headquarters in the afternoon. BRIELEN shelled with H.E. Enemy T.M's and shrapnel over EALING, SKIPTON, LANCASHIRE FARM, GOWTHORPE&OP. | |
| | 9th. | | Enemy aircraft active in the morning registering on Gun Positions and BAGNANI. G.O.C. at CASSEL representing Corps Commander at funeral of Italian General BAGNANI. | |
| | 10th. | | Enemy aircraft active. 5th Belgian Division on our left relieved by 6th Belgian Division. GENERAL DE CEUNMCK, Commanding 6th Belgian Division, called on G.O.C. Enemy Artillery quiet. | |
| | 11th. | | Enemy T.M's active on SKIPTON, THE NILE, and EALING. Slight shelling of ELVERDINGHE. | |
| | 12th. | | Enemy Trench Mortars and Artillery shelled BOESINGHE and support line in the afternoon. | |
| | 13th. | | Our Artillery and Stokes Mortars retaliated. ELVERDINGHE shelled between 5 p.m. and midnight. | |
| | 14th. | | Effective bombardment of enemy line opposite centre Brigade. O.O. 81 issued. | App: I |
| | 15th. | | Enemy raided two of our posts near TURCO FARM under cover of intense artillery and T.M. bombardment, killing one man, wounding four, and taking three prisoners and a Lewis Gun. We bombarded One German left dead in our trenches. Our artillery retaliated vigorously. We bombarded HIGH COMMAND during the day and Germans bombarded LA BRIQUE and in the evening shelled ROUSSEL FARM heavily with 5.9. Battalion billeted there moved out into CARDOEN FARM, and 'L' Line. ELVERDINGHE CHATEAU also shelled. G.O.C. visited H.Q. of 6th Belgian Division. Enemy aeroplane brought down in flames near ELVERDINGHE. | App: II |
| | 16th. | | Our artillery active. O.O. 82 issued. | |
| | 17th. | | Quiet day. | /Raid on |

1875  W: W593/826  1,000,000  4/15  J.B.C. & A.  A.D.S.S./Forms/C. 2118.

Army Form C. 2118

Page 2.

# WAR DIARY
## INTELLIGENCE SUMMARY

Instructions regarding War Diaries and Intelligence Summaries are contained in F.S. Regs., Part II. and the Staff Manual respectively. Title Pages will be prepared in manuscript.

| Place | Date | Hour | Summary of Events and Information | Remarks and references to Appendices |
|---|---|---|---|---|
| ST SIXTE. | FEBRUARY 18th. | | Raid on enemy line at U.14.a.3.4. by party of 14th Royal Welsh Fusiliers. Enemy Front Trenches badly battered by our artillery fire and evacuated by enemy, who placed barrage on them after raiders had entered. No prisoners taken, and no identifications secured. | App III |
| | 19th. | | The Army Commander, SIR HERBERT PLUMER visited the G.O.C.  Quiet day. | |
| | 20th. | | Quiet day. | |
| | 21st. | | Enemy Trench Mortar activity against our posts in Left section wrecking one post. | |
| | 22nd. | | Little artillery activity. | |
| | 23rd. | | G.O.C. proceeded on leave and Brigadier-General T.O. MARDEN, C.M.G. took over command. Brigadier-General MARDEN at Army Headquarters.  Quiet day. | |
| | 24th. | | Enemy T.M. activity on left section and left of centre section.  Our Artillery retaliated. | |
| | 25th. | | Enemy raided post in C.14.9. and carried off Sergeant and Lewis Gun.  Enemy bombardment inflicted heavy casualties on our supports and working parties.  Our Artillery barraged ARUPP and retaliated for enemy fire. | |
| | 26th. | | Enemy shelled Left Section and ELVERDINGHE.  O.O. 83 issued. | |
| | 27th. | | Some hostile shelling on centre section.  During night southern boundary of Divisional area readjusted. | |
| | 28th. | | Left Brigade front heavily bombarded with Artillery and Trench Mortars in the afternoon. | |

4/2/17.

[signature]
2nd Lieut.
General Staff 38th (Welsh) Division.

SECRET

GENERAL STAFF
HEADQUARTERS
8th CORPS.

No. G.510
Date ..........

38th Division No. G.S. 4160

VIII Corps

REPORT ON RAID BY THE GERMANS ON C.14.9
ON THE NIGHT 24th/25th FEBRUARY 1917.

The raid opened at 3 a.m. on the 25th instant with a heavy bombardment of the front line between EALING and FUSILIER TRENCH, and a box barrage formed immediately which included EALING TRENCH, FUSILIER TRENCH, MIRFIELD TRENCH and HEADINGLY LANE. In addition the Germans bombarded our front trench on both flanks of the area raided.

After about 2 minutes fire the bombardment on the front line was lifted and a party of Germans, estimated at about 50, broke through the front line near EALING TRENCH, and sweeping to the East captured one Sergeant and one Lewis Gun. Their stay in our lines was short as they left in about a couple of minutes.

Lewis Gun fire was brought to bear from both flanks on the raiders as they retired, but owing to the mist it has been impossible to say whether any were killed or not.

The hostile bombardment was kept up for about half an hour, and was replied to by our Artillery.

Our losses, which were all due to Artillery fire, were 3 Officers and 9 Other Ranks killed and 28 Other Ranks wounded.

It was unfortunate that one of the first shells of the enemy killed three Officers of the Support Company near LANCASHIRE FARM.

The heaviest losses were amongst a working party in FUSILIER TRENCH. and No dead Germans have been found in our lines, and no identifications have been ~~found~~.obtained.

25/2/1917.  
Brigadier General,  
Commanding 38th (Welsh) Division.

SS.143/9.

38th Div Arty Instructions & Orders

Vol. 16.

General Staff.
38th Division.
~~Final~~
~~History 1917~~

On His Majesty's Service.

Army Form C. 2118.

Vol 16

# WAR DIARY OF 38TH (WELSH) DIVISION.

General Staff.

## INTELLIGENCE SUMMARY

VOLUME XVI.

Instructions regarding War Diaries and Intelligence Summaries are contained in F. S. Regs., Part II. and the Staff Manual respectively. Title Pages will be prepared in manuscript.

| Place | Date | Hour | Summary of Events and Information | Remarks and references to Appendices |
|---|---|---|---|---|
| ST SIXTE. | March 1917 | | | |
| | 1st. | | ELVERDINGHE and battery positions in neighbourhood heavily shelled. Otherwise quiet. | |
| | 2nd. | | Enemy T.M. activity on Right Brigade front. Otherwise quiet day. | |
| | 3rd. | | Quiet day. | |
| | 4th. | | Quiet day except for shelling of battery positions. O. O. 84 issued. | App. I. |
| | 5th. | | Quiet day. | |
| | 6th. | | Enemy T.M. activity on front line in Right Brigade area. | |
| | 7th. | | Brigadier-General O.S.W. HICKIE relinquishes command of 115th Infantry Brigade. | |
| | 8th. | | Battery positions shelled. Otherwise quiet. | |
| | 9th. | | Brigadier-General J.K. MINSHULL FORD, D.S.O., M.C., assumes command of the 115th Infantry Brigade. O. O. 85 issued. | App. II. |
| | 10th. | | Major-General C.G. BLACKADER, C.B., D.S.O., A.D.C., returns from leave. Quiet day. Brigadier-General T.O. MARDEN relinquishes command of the Division and returns to 114th Infy. Brigade. Night 10/11th, 114th Infantry Brigade relieves 113th Infantry Brigade in the front line. | |
| | 11th. | | Quiet day. | |
| | 12th. | | Considerable shelling of CANAL BANK during the day. | |
| | 13th. | | Corps Commander visits Left Group, Artillery. | |
| | 14th. | | Quiet day. Conference of Brigadiers at REIGERSBURG CHATEAU. | |
| | 15th. | | Enemy T.M's active on Right Brigade front, and some shelling of back areas. | |
| | 16th. | | Quiet day. | |
| | 17th. | | Some registration on Right Brigade front. | |
| | 18th. | | Quiet day. | |
| | 19th. | | 4.30.a.m. Heavy bombardment of WILLOWS and TURCO: S.O.S. sent up and our artillery replied. No Infantry action took place. O. O. 86 issued. | |
| | 20th. | | Some artillery activity on battery positions in the vicinity of ELVERDINGHE. 113th Infantry Brigade move to BOLLEZEELE, being relieved in "D" Camp and "L" Lines by the 68th Infantry Brigade. | App. III. |
| | 21st. | | Enemy artillery very active on battery positions and back areas. Centre section of 2 battalions created, with Lieut-Colonel J. HAYES, D.S.O., in command. | |
| | 22nd. | | 4.30.a.m. Enemy raided our line in C.14.a. after a heavy bombardment, and although immediately ejected, succeeded in securing 3 prisoners. Some casualties also caused by the bombardment. | |
| | 23rd. | | Some shelling on front areas. | |
| | 24th. | | ELVERDINGHE shelled, otherwise quiet. | |
| | 25th. | | Quiet day. | |
| | | | | /26th. |

2449 Wt. W14957/M90 750,000 1/16 J.B.C. & A. Forms/C.2118/12.

Army Form C. 2118.

# WAR DIARY
## INTELLIGENCE SUMMARY

Page 2.

| Place | Date | Hour | Summary of Events and Information | Remarks and references to Appendices |
|---|---|---|---|---|
| | March 1917 | | | |
| ST SIXTE. | 26th. | | Slight shelling on Left Brigade front. | |
| | 27th. | | Quiet day. 173th Machine Gun Company joins the Division as 4th Machine Gun Company. | |
| | 28th. | | Quiet day. O.O. 87 issued. | |
| | 29th. | | Quiet day. | |
| | 30th. | | Mutual artillery bombardment on Right and Centre sections fronts at 4.0.a.m., but no infantry action. | App. IV. |
| | | | 12 midnight - successful raid on west face of MORTELDJE SALIENT by party of the 15th Welsh Regt. 1 prisoner of 185th I. R. captured, and a number of Germans killed. Our casualties very slight. On night of 30/31st, 113th Infantry Brigade relieved 114th Infantry Brigade in the front line. Lieut-Colonel C.C. NORMAN assumed command of the Centre (ZWAANHOF) Section. | |
| | 31st. | | Some shelling of forward areas. | |

5/4/17.

C.Huxley
Captain,
General Staff 38th (Welsh) Division.

Vol. 17.

General Staff.
38th Division.
April 1917.

(6339) Wt. W160/M3016 1,500,000 10/17 McA & W Ltd (E1898) Forms W3091.   Army Form W.3091.

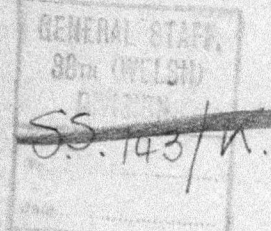

S.S.143/N.

# Cover for Documents.

**Nature of Enclosures.**

XIII Corps Orders & Instrns.

---

**Notes, or Letters written.**

WAR DIARY of GENERAL STAFF 38TH (WELSH) DIVISION. Army Form C. 2118.

Original

INTELLIGENCE SUMMARY

VOLUME XVII.

(Erase heading not required.)

| Place | Date | Hour | Summary of Events and Information | Remarks and references to Appendices |
|---|---|---|---|---|
| ST SIXTE. | APRIL 1917. | | | |
| | 1st. | | Slight artillery activity against the Right Section. | |
| | 2nd. | | The G.O.C. VIII Corps visited the Left Section. Weather cold with some snow. | |
| | 3rd. | | Slight hostile artillery activity against the CANAL BANK. | |
| | 4th. | | Slight hostile artillery activity against the Right Sector. | |
| | 5th. | | Situation quiet. Slight hostile artillery activity against the Right Sector. | app 1 |
| | | | Situation quiet. The 38th Divisional Sniping Coy. had a very successful day, and claims to have shot 10 Germans. | |
| | 6th. | | Quiet day. Nothing to report. O.O. 88 issued. | |
| | 7th. | | Situation quiet. A deserter of the 86th R.I.R. came over to our lines, and supplied much useful information. He said that 18th Reserve Division has left the sector opposite the 38th (Welsh) Division, and had gone to neighbourhood of ARRAS. | |
| | 8th. | | Situation quiet. Nothing to report. | |
| | 9th. | | Slight hostile activity against DAWSON CITY. | |
| | 10th. | | Slight hostile shelling in the region of HUDDERSFIELD ROAD and CANAL BANK in O.19.c. | |
| | 11th. | | Situation quiet. Nothing to report. | |
| | 12th. | | Situation normal. | |
| | 13th. | | Nothing to report. Situation normal. | |
| | 14th. | | Situation quiet. The Division had a test gas alarm. | |
| | 15th. | | Situation quiet. Weather very bad. O.O. 89 issued. | app 2 |
| | 16th. | | Situation quiet. Captain A.C.T. EVANSON, 176th Machine Gun Company, attached to "G" as Divisional Machine Gun Officer. | |
| | 17th. | | Situation quiet. 39th Division took over the sector occupied by the Right Battalion of the 38th (Welsh) Division. | app 3 |
| | 18th. | | Situation quiet. Weather very bad. O.O. 90 issued. | |
| | 19th. | | Situation normal. | |
| | 20th. | | Hostile artillery active against the CANAL BANK. | |
| | 21st. | | Major-General C.H. HARINGTON, M.G., G.S. Second Army, visited 38th Division Headquarters. | |
| | | | Situation quiet. | |
| | 22nd. | | Situation quiet. 113th Infantry Brigade relieved 114th Infantry Brigade in the line. | |
| | 23rd. | | The enemy made a gas attack on the French near NIEUPORT: the effects were slightly felt in the back areas of the Division. Lieut-General MICHEL, G.O.C., 4th Belgian Division visited 38th Divisional Headquarters. All quiet on the Divisional front. | |

/24th.

Army Form C. 2118

# WAR DIARY
## INTELLIGENCE SUMMARY
*(Erase heading not required.)*

PAGE 2.

| Place | Date | Hour | Summary of Events and Information | Remarks and references to Appendices |
|---|---|---|---|---|
| ST SIXTE. | APRIL 1917. | | | |
| | 24th. | | Our artillery active against the enemy. Hostile artillery opened a bombardment of our line during the night 24/25th. No infantry action followed. | Opp 4. |
| | 25th. | | Our artillery active against the enemy's line during the day. O.O. 91 issued. | |
| | 26th. | | Slight artillery activity against SKIPTON POST. | |
| | 27th. | | Our artillery active wire-cutting and bombarding the KRUPP SALIENT. The G.O.C. and G.S.O.1. attended a Conference at VIII Corps Headquarters (CHATEAU LOVIE). | |
| | 28th. | | Some hostile artillery activity against THE NILE, EALING TRENCH, LANCASHIRE FARM, Our artillery continued to bombard the KRUPP SALIENT. | |
| | 29th. | | The enemy retaliated heavily on the Right Brigade front for our shelling. Dummy raid on the enemy's line in the KRUPP SALIENT. | |
| | 30th. | | Very successful raid by the 15th Battalion, Welsh Regt on the enemy's line in C.15.c. (CALENDAR TRENCH). Many casualties inflicted on the enemy. One machine gun and 10 prisoners belonging to the 392nd Infantry Regiment captured. Our casualties were very light. | |
| | 15/5/17. | | | |

G. Drake-Brockman
Captain,
General Staff 38th (Welsh) Division.

CONFIDENTIAL                                      G.H.Q. O.B./2015

Fifth Army
---------

It has been observed that there is a tendency in some formations to circulate copies of operation orders and instructions than is often warranted by the nature or contents of the order.

Cases have occurred where copies of secret instructions, such as those relating to a special artillery operation, have been issued to the Chemical Advisor, the Provost Marshal, the A.D.Tn. the A.D.L., etc. From this it would seem that the copies of such orders or instructions are issued in some cases automatically, according to a general list kept in the office, without reference to the contents of the order or sufficient consideration as to whom it concerns.

It is an important and necessary duty of the Staff of all formations to review the method of issuing secret instructions and to ensure that as few copies of operation orders or secret instructions as possible are issued, and that they are only issued to those concerned.

In this connection it should be borne in mind that at the Headquarters of any formation there are some Officers who only require information on certain points. It should seldom be necessary or advisable to issue copies of the complete operation orders to such Officers, e.g., those in the administrative services and departments. These Officers should receive their instructions or information by means of extracts from the operation orders imparted either in writing or verbally - as may be most expedient - by the branch of the Staff concerned.

Whilst recognising that "the actual form of an order is of little importance" (F.S.R. Part I, Chap II, 12.4), when a formal operation order is issued a distinction should always be made in the detail of copies issued as regards the addressees to whom a copy of the order is sent for information only. Where operation instructions or memorandum are issued in lieu of formal operation orders, the most convenient method is to state at the top the Units or formations to which the order is addressed for action, and at the foot the Units or formations or Officers to which copies are forwarded for information.

General Headquarters,                         (sd) L.E. KIGGELL,
5th April 1917.                                    Lieut. General,
                                                       C.G.S.

C O N F I D E N T I A L                                G.H.Q. O.B./2015

Fifth Army
---------

It has been observed that there is a tendency in some formations to circulate copies of operation orders and instructions than is often warranted by the nature or contents of the order.

Cases have occurred where copies of secret instructions, such as those relating to a special artillery operation, have been issued to the Chemical Adviser, the Provost Marshal, the A.D.Tn. the A.D.L., etc. From this it would seem that the copies of such orders or instructions are issued in some cases automatically, according to a general list kept in the office, without reference to the contents of the order or sufficient consideration as to whom it concerns.

It is an important and necessary duty of the Staff of all formations to review the method of issuing secret instructions and to ensure that as few copies of operation orders or secret instructions as possible are issued, and that they are only issued to those concerned.

In this connection it should be borne in mind that at the Headquarters of any formation there are some Officers who only require information on certain points. It should seldom be necessary or advisable to issue copies of the complete operation orders to such Officers, e.g., those in the administrative services and departments. Those Officers should receive their instructions or information by means of extracts from the operation orders imparted either in writing or verbally - as may be most expedient - by the branch of the Staff concerned.

Whilst recognising that "the actual form of an order is of little importance" (F.S.R. Part I, Chap II, 12.4), when a formal operation order is issued a distinction should always be made in the detail of copies issued as regards the addressees to whom a copy of the order is sent for information only. Where operation instructions or memorandum are issued in lieu of formal operation orders, the most convenient method is to state at the top the Units or formations to which the order is addressed for action, and at the foot the Units or formations or Officers to which copies are forwarded for information.

General Headquarters,                         (sd) L.E. KIGGELL,
5th April 1917.                                    Lieut. General,
                                                       C.G.S.

CONFIDENTIAL                                G.H.Q. O.B./2015

Fifth Army
---------

It has been observed that there is a tendency in some formations to circulate copies of operation orders and instructions than is often warranted by the nature or contents of the order.

Cases have occurred where copies of secret instructions, such as those relating to a special artillery operation, have been issued to the Chemical Advisor, the Provost Marshal, the A.D.Tn. the A.D.L., etc. From this it would seem that the copies of such orders or instructions are issued in some cases automatically, according to a general list kept in the office, without reference to the contents of the order or sufficient consideration as to whom it concerns.

It is an important and necessary duty of the Staff of all formations to review the method of issuing secret instructions and to ensure that as few copies of operation orders or secret instructions as possible are issued, and that they are only issued to those concerned.

In this connection it should be borne in mind that at the Headquarters of any formation there are some Officers who only require information on certain points. It should seldom be necessary or advisable to issue copies of the complete operation orders to such Officers, e.g., those in the administrative services and departments. These Officers should receive their instructions or information by means of extracts from the operation orders imparted either in writing or verbally - as may be most expedient - by the branch of the Staff concerned.

Whilst recognising that "the actual form of an order is of little importance" (F.S.R. Part I, Chap II, 12.4), when a formal operation order is issued a distinction should always be made in the detail of copies issued as regards the addressees to whom a copy of the order is sent for information only. Where operation instructions or memorandum are issued in lieu of formal operation orders, the most convenient method is to state at the top the Units or formations to which the order is addressed for action, and at the foot the Units or formations or Officers to which copies are forwarded for information.

General Headquarters,             (sd) L.E. KIGGELL,
5th April 1917.                        Lieut. General,
                                            C.G.S.

Vol. 18.

General Staff.
38th Division.
May 1917.

~~Secret~~

SS 143/F

~~III Corps Artillery Instructions~~

S. SECRET

(6339) Wt. W160/M3016 1,500,000 10/17 McA & W Ltd (E1898) Forms W3091.    Army Form W.3091.

## Cover for Documents.

**Nature of Enclosures.**

(1) Defensive Measures by General Foch.
  V Corps G.x. 3715 23/6/18

(2) Army Comdr's Conference on
  V Corps. G.x. 3695/1 28/6/18

---

**Notes, or Letters written.**

# WAR DIARY
## INTELLIGENCE SUMMARY

*(Erase heading not required.)*

Army Form C. 2118

Page 2.

Instructions regarding War Diaries and Intelligence Summaries are contained in F.S. Regs., Part II. and the Staff Manual respectively. Title Pages will be prepared in manuscript.

| Place | Date | Hour | Summary of Events and Information | Remarks and references to Appendices |
|---|---|---|---|---|
| ST SIXTE. | MAY 1917. | | | |
| | 17th. | | A.A.&.Q.M.G. returns from leave. Attempted enterprise by 114th Infantry Brigade. Intelligence Officer visited the line in the LANCASHIRE FARM Sector, also 39th Divisional H.Q. Intelligence Officer interrogates German prisoners. False gas alarm. | |
| | 19th. | | H.O.C. and Intelligence Officer visit the line. Quiet day. 39th Division sent up S.O.S. signal during the night. No action followed. Completion of Brigade relief. 115th Infantry Brigade moved into Left Section, 114th Infantry Brigade sideslipped into Right Section, and 113th Infantry Brigade moved to Training Area round HOUTKERQUE. | |
| | 20th. | | Nothing to report. | |
| | 21st. | | G.O.C. visited the line in the LANCASHIRE FARM Sector, G.SMO's 1, 2 and 3 visited the line. | |
| | 22nd. | | Nothing to report. | |
| | 23rd. | | Nothing to report. | |
| | 24th. | | G.S.O.3. visited the training area in HERZEELE. Trench Mortar shoot postponed. | |
| | 25th. | | G.O.C. proceeded on leave to BOULOGNE. CAPTAIN N.J. HARINGTON, B.S.O., West Yorks Regt, takes over duties of G.S.O.3. 38th Division, vice CAPTAIN G.P.L.DRAKE BROCKMAN, M.C. Trench Mortar bombardment of enemy's lines opposite BOESINGHE Sector. | |
| | 26th. | | New trenches successfully dug in NO MANS LAND from C.14.10. to C.13.3. Only 3 casualties. G.S.O.3 and new G.S.O.3. visited 114th and 115th Infantry Brigades. | |
| | 27th. | | C.R.A. went to ARRAS to see Tank Scheme. Situation quiet. Wind S.E. | |
| | 28th. | | About 3.0.a.m. a gas alarm was received. Within a few minutes it was reported to be a false alarm. CAPTAIN DRAKE BROCKMAN, M.C., joined 57th Infantry Brigade as Brigade Major. Corps Commander visited trenches and Observation Posts during the afternoon, accompanied by G.S.O.1. CAPTAIN A.SMITH, M.C., G.S.O.2. left the Division to take up duty as G.S.O.2. Operations XIV Corps. MAJOR R.B. FOLLETT, D.S.O., Rifle Brigade, took over duty as G.S.O.2. G.O.C. returned from leave. | |
| | 29th. | | 113th Infantry Brigade moved to NOORDPEENE AREA. G.S.O.1., D.M.G.O., and Intelligence Officer went to ARRAS to see Tank Scheme. Situation quiet. | |
| | 30th. | | G.O.C., B.G.GMS., H.R.H., THE PRINCE OF WALES, and G.S.O.1. went round the line in the morning. KING ALBERT OF BELGIUM visited the Left Sector, and afterwards telephoned to express his pleasure at the good feeling between the English and Belgians in the trenches. G.S.O.2., G.S.O.3., and D.M.G.O. visited the Right Sector in the afternoon. Our Artillery in conjunction with Trench Mortars and M.G's carried out a practive barrage. 113th Infantry Brigade completed move to QUELMES Training Area. | |
| | 31st. | | | |

T.J. Harington Captain
General Staff 38th (Welsh) Division.

Army Form C. 2118.

# WAR DIARY
## INTELLIGENCE SUMMARY

*(Erase heading not required.)*

GENERAL STAFF 38TH (WELSH) DIVISION.

VOLUME XVIII.

Instructions regarding War Diaries and Intelligence Summaries are contained in F. S. Regs., Part II. and the Staff Manual respectively. Title Pages will be prepared in manuscript.

| Place | Date | Hour | Summary of Events and Information | Remarks and references to Appendices |
|---|---|---|---|---|
| ST SIXTE. | MAY 1917. 1st. | | Quiet day except for hostile shelling of DAWSONS CORNER. Relief of 115th Infantry Brigade by 114th Infantry Brigade in the BOESINGHE SECTOR. 115th Infantry Brigade move to Training Area BOLLEZEELE. | |
| | 2nd. | | Hostile artillery shelled FAERDY FARM in the morning, otherwise quiet. Corps Commander visited Divisional Headquarters. G.S.O.3. proceeded to Second Army Intelligence. Intelligence Officer visited the line, and inspected tracks in the 38th Divisional Area. | |
| | 3rd. | | G.O.C. 4th Belgian Division visited G.O.O. G.S.O.3. returns from Second Army Intelligence. | |
| | 4th. | | Nothing to report. | |
| | 5th. | | ELVERDINGHE CHATEAU and grounds heavily shelled during the night, also Divisional Ammunition Column, and POPERINGHE. | |
| | 6th. | | Quiet day. Hostile raid C.13.3. at 2.30.a.m. Three of 13th Royal Welsh Fusiliers missing. G.S.O.3. visited Belgian G.H.Q.; also Belgian line. ELVERDINGHE CHATEAU and grounds again heavily shelled during the night. | |
| | 7th. | | We retaliated for the hostile shelling of our back areas, by 2 rapid bursts of 5 minutes each from our artillery. Second Army Heavy artillery shelled enemy billets and back areas. | |
| | 8th. | | Quiet day. G.S.O.1. and G.S.O.2. and Intelligence Officer visited the line. CAPTAIN L.A. BRIERLEY arrives as Brigade Major 113th Infantry Brigade vice CAPTAIN L.C. MacD.STEWART wounded. | |
| | 9th. | | Quiet day. G.S.O.3. visited the line. G.S.O.1. proceeded on leave. | |
| | 10th. | | Quiet day. | |
| | 11th. | | G.O.C. and G.S.O.2. visited the Training Area at BOLLEZEELE. | |
| | 12th. | | G.O.C. visited the trenches. Intelligence Officer visited tracks in the evening. Very frosty. G.S.O.2. visited the Left Area in the morning. Intelligence Officer interrogated prisoners. | |
| | 13th. | | Quiet day. Thunderstorm in the night. Belgian balloon brought down in flames. Belgian Officers visited Divisional Headquarters. | |
| | 14th. | | Nothing to report. Intelligence Officer interrogated prisoners. Unsuccessful raid by enemy. G.S.O.C. visited the line. | |
| | 15th. | | Intelligence Officer visited the line in the morning, and Sniping Coy in the evening. G.S.O.2. visited Divisional School. O.O.92 issued for Brigade relief. Cold day. Intelligence Officer reconnoitring for training areas. | |
| | /17th. | | | App. 1 /17th. |

S E C R E T.

Headquarters,

114 Infantry Brigade.

---

I beg to forward the following report on the operation carried out on the night of the 29/30th April by a special party under the command of Captain J.A.DANIEL, of the Battalion under my command.

1. **PRELIMINARY TRAINING.**

   In accordance with the Scheme dated 19th April the party under Captain J.A.DANIEL assembled at BURGOMASTER FARM on the 22nd April and commenced training on the following day. Their training was divided into two main heads.

   (a) Training for Offensive Action in accordance with "Instructions for training of Platoons" and Training to make them fit for hard work.
   (b) Special Training by day and by night on a replica of the portion of the hostile trenches to be attacked.

   During the above period all Officers and N.C.O's and a proportion of the men went out by night to examine the ground over which they would have to attack and to familiarise themselves with the landmarks and guiding points in the enemy line.

   To the careful instruction given by Captain DANIEL and his Officers and the keenness and attention paid by all ranks during their preliminary training and instruction, I attribute in a very great measure the ultimate success of the operation. Too much attention cannot be paid to preliminary training and instruction in the most minute detail.

2. **NARRATIVE OF RAID.**

   On the night of the raid a special patrol was sent out after the Dummy raid from 9-30 p.m. to 10 p.m. to ascertain if the enemy was still holding his line as owing to his inactivity for several days previously, it was feared that he might have evacuated his trenches.

   The Officer i/c of the patrol reported at 11-25 p.m. that the enemy was not only holding his line in what appeared to be a normal manner, but had a wiring party at work near NO MAN'S COT. (C.15.c.7.7.). This party was evidently caught by our Artillery Fire as at least four dead were seen at this point when the raiding party attacked. The message "BRIDGE" (Operation will be carried out) was accordingly sent to Brigade Headquarters and the Artillery at 11-26 p.m..

   At 10-5 p.m. the party laying tapes and marking the assembly position commenced work and completed the same by 11-40 p.m. This took a little longer than was anticipated owing to occasional bursts of hostile M.G. fire and the presence of the enemy wiring party above referred to which was only a short distance from the left of the assembly position and could be clearly seen as the night was then very clear and still. The salvo fired by our Artillery at 10-45 p.m. was of great assistance, as it drove the enemy wiring party in and prevented our party from being spotted by them, and under cover of the smoke that drifted back the tapes to the left of the assembly position were rapidly run out.

The Raiding Party left the rendezvous at CONEY STREET at 11 p.m. moving in two columns in accordance with Operation Orders. The Right Column was obliged to make a detour from BOUNDARY ROAD in order to reach the front line, owing to hostile shelling of BOUNDARY ROAD near the point where it crosses the WILLOWS DRAIN (C.21.a.25.80). This column was consequently a few minutes late in arriving at its point of exit from our front line, but this did not interfere with the move to the Assembly Position, and the whole of the raiding party was in position on the line at 12-7 a.m.

At 12-18 a.m. the message "WHITE" (All ready) was received at Report Centre and transmitted at once to Brigade Headquarters, and to the Artillery.

At 12-29 a.m. the feint bombardment commenced and at 12-30 a.m. simultaneously with the real bombardment the message "RED" (Advance has commenced) was received at Report Centre. At 12-42 a.m. the message "BROWN" (2nd Wave in trenches) was received at Report Centre.

During the advance from the Assembly Position formations were well kept on the whole, though there was a slight tendency to crowd in to the centre. The "going" was found to be good and free from obstacles, except on the extreme right, where the Bombing Section of the 1st Wave encountered the wire round Sap 16. This only caused a momentary check and the advance was continued up to within 40 or 50 yards of our barrage, when a halt lasting about half a minute was necessary in order to allow the bombardment to lift on to the Support Line.

The 1st Wave actually crossed the enemy's front line at 12.34 a.m. and the 2nd Wave was in the front line by 12.35 a.m. One man of ours was killed on the Front Line parapet just as the 1st Wave crossed the Front Line.

The 1st Wave halted for about half a minute after crossing the enemy front line to allow the barrage to lift and also the parties composing it to close up. The objective of the 1st Wave (viz. CALENDAR SUPPORT) was reached and all parties were in position at XXX 12.37 a.m.

The parties of the 2nd Wave were in position at 12-34 a.m. and the Green light fired at 12-37 a.m. by O.C. Raid.

The 1st Wave met with no opposition whatsoever except on the extreme left where a small party of bombers was encountered and driven back up the trench to MULLER COT into our barrage, and the enemy support was found to be unoccupied.

Very Lights and Red Lights were fired from the Reserve

Line which was occupied, and from which a counterattack might
have developed had it not been for the excellence of the
Artillery barrage and the action of the Lewis Gun Section
(Party S.) with No.1 Platoon taking up a position on the
Support Line from which it fired on the Reserve Line and
kept down the heads of the enemy occupying it, and also
the Communication Trenches to the Right and Left, viz:-
CALENDAR LANE and the trench running towards MULLER COT.

The 2nd Wave found the Front Line occupied and met with
a certain amount of opposition, mainly from men in dugouts,
which was quickly overcome and the whole of the garrison
of the Front Line either killed or taken prisoners.
Shortly before 1 a.m. 2/Lieut. I.S.MORGAN, Commanding No.2
Platoon, was wounded, but carried on in command of his
Platoon and returned with it to our lines.

The work of clearing the trenches inside the barrage
was completed shortly after 1 a.m. and the order to with-
draw sent by runner to the Support Line, and the withdrawal
of the 1st Wave through the enemy front line was carried out
as arranged. The 2nd Wave withdrew immediately after,
according to orders, and the whole party re-formed at the
original Assembly Position by 1-10 a.m. At 1-45 a.m. the
Raiding Party withdrew to our lines and was re-assembled at
CONEY STREET by 2 a.m. The whole withdrawal was carried out
in an orderly manner and the behaviour of the men was
excellent in every way.

## 3. ARTILLERY & T.M. FIRE.

(a) Our Artillery and Stokes Mortar fire was extremely
accurate and well timed and the success of the raid is due
to a very great extent to this.

No alterations in the barrages were found necessary as
far as the raiding party was concerned and our fire died down
at ZERO plus 50 as previously arranged.

(b) Enemy's Artillery retaliation was comparatively light;
his Trench Mortars were, however, very active from HIGH
COMMAND REDOUBT against our own trenches. His Light Trench
Mortars from the direction of MULLER COT fired on the ground
between CALENDAR SUPPORT but without any serious effect, and
in no way hindering our operations. A hostile Machine Gun
from CANADIAN FARM fired during most of the raid, but this
also in no way hindered our operations. No other hostile
Machine Guns were heard firing at all.

## 4. INFORMATION re TRENCHES.

The enemy's trenches were much knocked about by our
bombardment; CALENDAR SUPPORT was mostly derelict and had the
appearance of not having been used for a considerable period.
There had been wire in front, but it was destroyed by shell
fire. The front line trench (CALENDAR TRENCH) was 6 to 7 feet
and revetted with brushwood hurdles and was fire-stepped along

N.C.O's and men who have been brought to my notice, as men deserving of immediate reward for their services. At the same time I consider that the whole hearted co-operation of every individual Officer, N.C.O. and man from the moment their training started until the operation was brought to a successful conclusion is deserving of the highest praise, and contributed very largely to their success. The men entered into the spirit of the whole operation like a team going into a football competition and were in the highest spirits from start to finish.

(sd) THOS. W. PARKINSON,
Lieut. Colonel,
Commanding 15th Welsh Regiment.

2nd May 1917.

C.1397.

SECRET.                                                    COPY NO. 12

To:-

Headquarters,

   38th (Welsh) Division.

_____

1.  I forward herewith reports marked A, B, and C, on the raids carried out by 15th and 13th Welsh on nights 29th/30th April, and 30th April/1st May.

2.  The raids were planned for 12th and 13th March. It was anticipated that stronger enemy resistance and a heavier barrage would be encountered, otherwise a deeper penetration and larger results could have been obtained. As it turned out, the raids could have been carried out equally successfully by a third of the numbers, but I am of opinion that the risk of casualties was more than counter-balanced by larger numbers who gained experience, and received careful training. The moral of the Battalions engaged and of the whole of the 114th Infantry Brigade has been heightened by the success of the raids.

3.  The well-known difficulty of keeping gaps in the wire open was well solved by O.C. Right Group R.A. (Colonel RUDKIN) who substituted wire-cutting on a large scale during the few days preceding the raids, instead of deliberate cutting. All the wire was practically swept away. Wire can no longer be considered an obstacle to an attack provided -
    (a) Wire-cutting can be properly observed.
    (b) Sufficient time to cut it can be given, an allowance being made for bad weather.
    (c) It is cut on a sufficiently broad front.

4.  The action of the German higher command shows both apathy and distrust of the offensive spirit of their troops. It was anticipated that their front line would be cleared, and their guns turned on to it, this being followed by a counter-attack. Consequently an advanced Officers Patrol was sent out for both raids to ascertain that the enemy was occupying his front trenches. The pocket barrage by Field Artillery and the action of counter-batteries was arranged on the above assumption. Though the Germans did not shell their own front line, except during the first portion of the dummy bombardment on KRUPP, the effect of the Field and        Heavy Artillery in subduing their Trench Mortar and Gun barrages was very marked.

5.  From examination of prisoners it has been ascertained that the 15th Welsh attacked on the frontage of a portion of the 7th Company, 392nd I.R., and the 13th Welsh on the frontage of portions of the 5th and 6th Companies. There should not have been more than about 30 men on the former and 40 on the latter. From the accounts of Officers and men of the numbers killed by our bombardment, and by raiders and by the number of prisoners

taken it is clear that the front trenches in the area raided were swept clean.

6. Great credit is due to Lieut.Colonel PARKINSON, D.S.O. Commanding 15th Welsh and Lieut.Colonel KENNEDY, M.C. Commanding 13th Welsh for the careful arrangement of the details which are such an essential factor in raids. The 15th Welsh, who moved up to their assembly positions via communication trenches, used with great success sandbags round their feet to deaden the noise of tramping on the duckboards. The 13th Welsh had to advance across country for 400 yards until they reached our outpost line, thence for another 100 yards to the assembly position, passing through our wire on route, thence for an average of 150 yards to the enemy's front trenches. The latter was carried out in 13 columns. There were no definite directing marks as in the case of the 15th Welsh, who had the MORTELDJE trees, and direction was maintained on the 400 yards frontage by connecting each column to the next by measured lengths of telephone wire. The two directing columns had each a telephone wire on the ground from the assembly position to an old trench which led direct to two salients. These were laid out two nights previously, and proved very successful.

7. The value of the following were again emphasised:-
   (1) Breaking the raiders up into small parties, each headed by an Officer or N.C.O. and each assigned a definite task.
   (2) Drill on a replica. The men seemed surprised to find dugouts etc. in the places where flags had been placed on the replica.
   (3) A liberal supply of large scale maps showing all available information. In this the Brigade were greatly assisted by Divisional Headquarters.

8. The patrol telephone supplied by the 38th Division was very useful, and the Power Buzzer was also used with success.

9. When once the raiders have started from the assembly position the only manner in which they can be assisted is by the manipulation of the Artillery. This was most efficiently done by Colonel RUDKIN, C.C. Right Group R.A. who relied for both raids on his information as to enemy barrage on his observer (Lieut. BROCKLEHURST, R.A.) at GOWTHORPE. This is the fourth raid for which Lieut. BROCKLE-HURST has observed and I beg to bring his name to the special notice of the Divisional Commander.

10. The Artillery work throughout, both of the Divisional and Heavy Artillery was excellent and gave the utmost confidence to the men. The system introduced by the O.C. Right Group of personally explaining the action of the Artillery to the raiders a few days before the raid is worthy of mention. The barrage was also practised on the replica by men carrying flags and by the use of drums.

11. A separate report on the condition of the enemy's trenches is attached, marked "D". I am of opinion that the blocks with steps in the trenches described in the report are not not intentional, but the result of our shelling, the steps being hastily made.

12. One of the new rockets - red changing to white - was used in each case for a withdrawal and was successful, though two at least failed to go off.

T.O.Marden.

Brigadier General,
Commanding 114th Infantry Brigade.

4th May 1917.


Copies to:-

No.1.) 38th
   2.) Division.
   3. O.C. Right Group.
   4. O.C. 10th Welsh.
   5.  "   13th   "
   6.  "   14th   "
   7.  "   15th   "
   8. 113th Infantry Brigade.
   9. 116th    "        "
  10. 118th    "        "
  11. War Diary.
  12. Office Copy.

REPORT ON TRENCHES RAIDED BY 13th Bn. THE WELSH REGT.

Appendix D

VON CLUCKS COTTAGES exist only as derelict dug-outs filled in.

The communication Trench from C.14.b.34.16 was in fairly good condition.

A mechanical bomb thrower was found in the front line S.E. of VON CLUCK COTTAGES.

At C.14.b.04.2. a concrete dug-out was found and blown up by the R.E.

At C.14.b.0.1½. a dug-out containing 8 Germans was found and blown up.

At C.14.b.¼.1. an emplacement consisting of a steel cupola was found smashed up by our Artillery. (Possibly a Sniper's Post or M.G.Emplacement).

At C.14.b.1.1½. a concrete structure with a steel dome was found. The front line trench was very good; 6 ft. to 7 ft. deep, dry and firestepped.

At C.14.b.7.2. a concrete dug-out was found and blown up by the R.E. This trench was in good repair and revetted with sandbags.

The entrance to CALABASH LANE C.14.b.8.1.3 had been blown in.

At C.14.b.5.3. a concrete dug-out had been destroyed by our Artillery.

At C.14.b.4½.2. a new concrete dug-out, practically completed, also one at C.14.b.4½.3½. were not dealt with.

At about C.14.b.6.6. there is apparently a strong point, as Very lights were sent up during the whole time the Raiders were in the trenches.

8 Germans were found dead in the trenches and 22 were killed by us.

**SECRET**

FILE No. **G.12.**

Sub-Nos. 176-

SUBJECT. *Minor Operations*

Sub-head. against HINDENBURG SUPPORT Line, by

19 R. Welsh Fus., 119th Bde., 40th Div. on

15 December 1917

~~VI Corps~~

| Referred to | Date. | Referred to | Date. |
|---|---|---|---|
| | | | |

Vol. 19.

General Staff.
38th Division.
June 1917.

ard Form C. 2118.

Instructions regarding War Diaries and Intelligence Summaries are contained in F. S. Regs., Part II. and the Staff Manual respectively. Title Pages will be prepared in manuscript.

# WAR DIARY

GENERAL STAFF 38TH (WELSH) DIVISION

## INTELLIGENCE SUMMARY

VOLUME XIX.

| Place | Date | Hour | Summary of Events and Information | Remarks and references to Appendices |
|---|---|---|---|---|
| ST SIXTE. | JUNE.1917. | | | |
| | 1st. | | G.S.O.1., G.S.O.2., and G.S.O.3. went round the line in the afternoon. Continued bombardment of enemy's trenches by Artillery and Trench Mortars. | |
| | 2nd. | | General Officer Commanding inspected Divisional school in the morning, and attended Corps Conference in the afternoon. Artillery carried out a practice barrage. Wind safe. | |
| | 3rd. | | Conference of Brigadiers. G.O.C., and G.S.O.1. visited the line to see practice barrage. ELVERDINGHE CHATEAU heavily shelled and Brigadier-General MINSHULL FORD wounded. | |
| | 4th. | | Our artillery continued the destructive and harassing shoot. Enemy retaliated on front and back areas. | |
| | 5th. | | Our artillery continued the destructive shoot, and carried out a practice barrage at 3.0.p.m. Corps Commander and G.S.O.1. went up the line in the afternoon. | |
| | 6th. | | Divisional Order No.93. issued for demonstration on Divisional front in conjunction with Southern offensive. | APP. 1 |
| | | | Our artillery continued destructive fire, which caused some retaliation. Prisoners of Successful raid by 16th Welsh Regt on night 5th/6th June across the CANAL. Slight retaliation. 2nd Battalion, 288th Landwehr Regt, taken. | |
| | 7th. | | All objectives in Southern offensive reached by 7.0.p.m. with 5650 prisoners. Our artillery Machine Guns and Trench Mortars fired from 3.10.a.m. throughout the day. Slight retaliation. Divisional Order No.94. issued in connection with further demonstration. | APP. 2 |
| | | | Divisional Order No.95 issued in connection with probable relief of 388th Landwehr Regt. | APP. 3 |
| | 8th. | | At 2.0.a.m. 500 cylinders of gas were successfully discharged, weather conditions being favourable. Our artillery opened fire at 2.30.a.m. according to programme. | |
| | 9th. | | A quiet day. Second and Fifth Army Commanders visited Divisional Headquarters, and afterwards went to 114th Brigade to see scheme for crossing CANAL on mats. Raid by 15th Welsh Regt: no result. | |
| DRAGON CAMP | | | Divisional Order No.96. issued in connection with relief of 114th Infantry Brigade by 113th Infantry Brigade in the LANCASHIRE FARM Section. 114th Infantry Brigade on relief proceed to Reserve Brigade Area. DRAGON. | APP. 4 |
| | | | 38th Divisional Headquarters, move into VOX VRIE CAMP. (Divisional Order No.97 issued). Enemy reported to be holding his front line very strongly. 113th Infantry Brigade arrived at POPERINGHE. | APP. 5 |
| | 11th. | | Between 3.a.m. and 4.a.m. enemy barraged our front line system very heavily: no action followed. Divisional Conference. 38th Division joined XIV Corps. | |
| | | | | 12th/ |

2449 Wt. W14957/M90 750,000 1/16 J.B.C. & A. Forms/C.2118/12.

Army Form C. 2118.

# WAR DIARY
## INTELLIGENCE SUMMARY

Page 2.

Instructions regarding War Diaries and Intelligence Summaries are contained in F.S. Regs, Part II. and the Staff Manual respectively. Title Pages will be prepared in manuscript.

| Place | Date | Hour | Summary of Events and Information | Remarks and references to Appendices |
|---|---|---|---|---|
| DRAGON CAMP. | JUNE.1917. 12th. | | 113th Infantry Brigade relieved 114th Infantry Brigade in the Right Sub-section. Enemy attempted to raid our trenches but was driven off, leaving the officer in charge and 2 men prisoners in our hands. | |
| | 13th. | | Divisional Order No.98 issued for relief of 115th Infantry Brigade by 2nd Guards Brigade. Guards Division arrived in Corps Area. | APP. 6 |
| | 14th. | | 38th Division side-slipped to a line drawn at Right-angles half way between BRIDGE 4 and 4.A. Enemy bombarded the vicinity of 'J' Camp at 3.0.a.m. No damage. Orders received from Corps to give up 'J' Camp to Guards Division. Divisional Order No.99 issued giving new boundary for 38th Division. Divisional School dispersed, and Instructors joined Reinforcement Camp at Camp 'H', pending further orders. Sniping Coy move to 'H' Camp. 2nd Guards Brigade take over BOESINGHE SECTION from 115th Infantry Brigade. Situation normal. Some hostile aerial activity. | APP. 7 |
| | 16th. | | Hostile artillery very active in the early morning. 14 hostile aeroplanes reported over our front system at 5.30; these were driven off and one seen to crash after a fight with our aeroplanes. Divisional Order No.100 issued in connection with relief of 10th Belgian Brigade by 2nd Guards Brigade. | APP. 8 |
| | 17th. | | Very quiet during the day and no hostile movement in front or back areas. Hostile artillery very active at night. | |
| | 18th. | | A quiet day, but some activity in the evening. Enemy shelled the vicinity of VOX VRIE FARM with H.V. gun. | |
| | 19th. | | Hostile artillery very active in the vicinity of ELVERDINGHE and CANAL BANK. About 9.45.p.m. two L.H.V. shells fell in DRAGON CAMP: No.1. close to the Canteen: No.2. immediately behind the C.O.'s Room. No damage. Divisional Order No.101 issued regarding Guards Division taking over command of the BOESINGHE SECTOR, with 2nd Guards Brigade in the front line. Hostile artillery fairly quiet during the day, but active towards the evening, increasing during the night. | APP. 9 |
| | 20th. | | The vicinity of DRAGON CAMP was shelled during the day: at 10.45. two L.H.V. shells fell in the camp killing two horses and wounding six, at the same time causing a fire in a hut. One man had his thumb blown off, otherwise no casualties. Divisional Order No.102 issued for move of 114th Infantry Brigade from BOESINGHE to TILQUES Training Area. 21st/. | APP. 10 |

Army Form C. 2118.

# WAR DIARY
## INTELLIGENCE SUMMARY
*(Erase heading not required)*

Page 3.

Instructions regarding War Diaries and Intelligence Summaries are contained in F. S. Regs., Part II and the Staff Manual respectively. Title Pages will be prepared in manuscript.

| Place | Date | Hour | Summary of Events and Information | Remarks and references to Appendices |
|---|---|---|---|---|
| DRAGON CAMP. | JUNE 1917. | | | |
| | 21st. | | Hostile artillery again active in the afternoon and evening on forward and back areas. Some of our battery positions were engaged. DRAGON CAMP and the vicinity were again engaged with a L.H.V. gun. A minor enterprise by the 113th Infantry Brigade succeeded in penetrating the hostile second line, but obtained no identifications. | |
| | 22nd. | | Some hostile activity on forward and back areas. L.H.V. gun fired on INTERNATIONAL CORNER and CORNISH CROSS ROADS during the day. Hostile aeroplane activity above normal. | |
| | 23rd. | | Hostile aeroplanes very active. Two of our balloons were brought down in flames. | |
| | 24th. | | Hostile artillery very active along the CANAL BANK. Several bridges destroyed and several direct hits on dugouts in this vicinity, causing some casualties. Divisional Order No.103 issued regarding move of 38th Division from DRAGON CAMP to the ST HILAIRE AREA. | APP. 11 |
| | 25th. | | Hostile artillery active on front and back areas. L.H.V. gun shelled PESELHOEK and area. North of VOX VRIE FARM. The Divisional Ammunition Column were shelled out of their lines about 9.p.m. Officers of 29th Division arrived at 38th Division headquarters to take over 38th Divisional Sector. Divisional Order No. 014 104 issued regarding relief of 38th Division by 29th Division in the ZWAANHOF SECTOR. | APP. 12 |
| | 26th. | | G.O.C., 29th Division arrived. CANAL BANK again shelled. Battery in vicinity of TROIS TOURS was engaged during the day. | |
| | 27th. | | A quiet morning, but heavy shelling of CANAL BANKS around BRIDGES 4 with 10.5.c.m. and 15.c.m. shells during the afternoon. Hostile aircraft displayed considerable activity. | |
| | 28th. | | During the night 27th/28th the enemy shelled the road between ESSEX CORNER and MARENGO HOUSE. The vicinity of DRAGON CAMP was again shelled during the day. On relief of 113th Infantry Brigade by 87th Infantry Brigade in the ZWAANHOF SECTOR. | |
| | 29th. | | 113th Infantry Brigade move to ST HILAIRE Training Area. Divisional Headquarters NORRENT FONTES. | |
| | 30th. | | 38th Division move to ST HILAIRE Training Area. Royal Engineers marking out replica of German trenches on the training area. Platoon Training. | |

Captain,
General Staff 38th (Welsh) Division.

SECRET

38th Division No. G.S.S.58/11.

## 38TH (WELSH) DIVISION OPERATIONS.
## DIVISION ORDER NO. 107.
### ADDENDUM.

To paragraph 7 ARTILLERY add new sub-para. after

(d) to be inserted after the word "Lines" Line 27 page 4.

    (e) The Creeping Barrage, which during the occupation of the BLUE, BLACK and GREEN Lines will have become temporarily stationary, will become intense for 4 minutes before it re-commences to creep so as to enable the attacking troops to get close to it.

ACKNOWLEDGE.

H.E. Pryce
Lieut. Colonel,
15-6-1917.    General Staff, 38th (Welsh) Division.

Copies to all recipients of D.O.107.

www.ingramcontent.com/pod-product-compliance
Lightning Source LLC
Chambersburg PA
CBHW081545160426
43191CB00011B/1842